Inducing Reality

The Holy Grail of Storytelling in Video Games

Ken Ramsley

Encellon Books

Encellon Books
ISBN: 9781973107248

Acknowledgments

Over the entire history of this project, I have greatly appreciated pointed suggestions. I particularly appreciate ongoing feedback, unvarnished critiques, and support from the *ttlg.com* community who motivated earlier editions and recent updates. Lastly, I am eternally grateful to Sue, my wife, who supports my creative work and offers a host of useful suggestions.

Acknowledgment

Contents

To the wizards of game design who turns stories into magic

Preface

Until you know how to tell a story *in general*, it is pointless to say much about storytelling in video games. If you're an expert storyteller, Chapter 7 is where you might begin. But if you're like the rest of us – still learning the storytelling craft – it might be wiser to start with Chapter 1.

Inducing Reality: The Holy Grail of Storytelling in Video Games was originally published on *ttlg.com* and other gaming websites. Working in a vacuum, design teams (including my own) lacked a clear sense of storytelling theory, and this was keeping us from prod–ucing a truly immersive game-playing experience. We knew that stories are important to games, but most game designers at the time did not understand the nuts-and-bolts of storytelling …a fact sadly still true in the present day. I do not say this as a criticism, nor am I going to pass judgment on every game produced today. Just like Maya, C++, motion-capture, and sound editing – producing a deeply immersive story is an acquired skill, and there's always a better way to tell a better story.

This book is about storytelling, *not* about word-selection, grammar, or punctuation. But I *can* say this about placing words on a page... Once I conjure a clearly stated premise, a collection of three-dimensional char–acters, a well-designed setting, and a quest that drives the story toward its conclusion ...as long as events are governed by the actions of my characters, and as long as I let the characters think for themselves – filling a page with text is rarely a problem.

To avoid all doubt, here is the premise of my book: *On the topic of producing a great story in any medium – human nature sets the only rules that matter.*

As you will discover in the text below, the hardwired rules of storytelling are *universal* and this handbook offers an equally useful introduction to stories in movie scripts, stage plays, novel-writing, and, of course ...video games. Obviously, if you are building a crossword puzzle app for iOS, you won't need to know much about storytelling. But if you are developing any sort of project based on human or humanlike characters ...read on. In the text that follows, I cover the essentials – plenty of food for thought ...enough for most writers starting out.

By nature, humans are built for storytelling, and more than anything else, I want to offer tools to help you enhance your natural storytelling abilities.

Ken Ramsley

Introduction

I appeal to all computer game project leaders, designers, and writers to consider the issue of the unchecked unsophistication in computer game stories and dialog very seriously and carefully.

– Richard "Zdim" Carlson

Having worked with dozens of development teams on hundreds of design projects across a host of professional fields, I can clearly see how the study of one's craft is easily shoved aside.

What is the solution?

We learn what we can absorb as time allows. But for this to happen, the material must arrive in an easily digestible format, and as it turns out, most books I've read on the topic of storytelling are long on self-promotion and short on useful details.

What if we had a handy storytelling manual written in bite-sized chunks designed to cover each topic in a few spare minutes? Each day, we could improve our skills without missing a beat.

That describes the format of this book.

So, let's get started!

There is perhaps one profession that predates the 'oldest profession' – storytelling. And it is no accident. Without the invention of storytelling, we wouldn't be reading books, watching movies, or playing video games on our lunch break. More than mere entertainment, the storyteller's skill is based on a powerful survival instinct – the ability to encode and transmit vast amounts of useful information by inducing a near-perfect sense of reality.

During most of *homo sapiens'* first 250,000 years on Earth, we had no written language. To pass information to the next generation, stories were stockpiled like a walking library. The tales would take early people on imaginary journeys, and along the way, their children would learn about which fruits to eat and which to avoid. How do we hunt monkeys high in the canopy? …the same as the story. Where do we find water in the dry season? …remember the story. All of this information was central to their survival, and our human capacity to relive a story in all of its many details kept its information alive.

As a matter of pure practicality, storytelling became central to our survival. Tribal families who told and remembered important stories prospered. Those who failed to pass critical information to the next generation lost their knowledge and faded away. At its core, storytelling is not about entertainment. Instead, the pleasure of a story is an evolutionary reward designed to keep us interested in the details of our practical survival. Even in our present-day books, movies, and video games, storytelling is still the best way to remember practical information, and people who remember lots of stories are usually the best problem-solvers. There's always a story that will offer a clue. In fact, the very roots of the word 'story' stem from the concept of a remembered history.

In a very deep way, humans are *hardwired* for stories. In fact, our instinct for stories is so strong, we often remember each story as though it were a genuine event in our lives. We are not spectators. We absorb stories as an intensely personal experience, and in this process, the lessons we learn are rooted in our thoughts to be recalled alongside our own personal histories. For the rest of our lives, to the same extent as real-life experiences, powerful stories shape our thoughts and emotions. Instead of books on a shelf, scenes on a screen, or people on a stage, they become parts of who we are.

But then, an odd thing happened on our way to human civilization. Someone noticed how stories could describe events that never happened in places that do not exist. Suddenly, a story could describe imaginary 'facts.' No one knows when fiction was invented. It very likely predates the written word. Yet ever since that day, fiction began to enter our thoughts, and we've been perturbed and enchanted by its power ever since.

Prior to fiction, a natural sequence of events told people how to tell a story. Storytellers talked about what happened, and they didn't bother to analyze why people preferred one story over another. People either valued what they learned from a story, or it was never told again.

On the other hand, professional fiction-writers typically create a boundless array of invented events with no natural connections to reality, and because of this, they cannot depend on natural events to govern the flow of a story. Without a natural flow of events, fiction-writers are on their own to invent the flow of the story for themselves.

They need to discover what makes some stories work, and others fail.

They need to understand the underlying rules of storytelling.

How do we produce a story?

Thankfully, Aristotle devoted considerable effort to the study of storytelling, and his written work forms the foundation of every textbook on the subject. According to Aristotle, our human hardwiring contains a number of fixed rules. Stories that follow the rules produce an immersive storytelling experience, and we ignore the rules at our peril.

What works is principally a matter of understanding how our audience experiences a story, and what can be done to induce an authentic immersive experience. Audiences are hardwired by 250,000 years of storytelling, and this programming sets the rules – not me, or any other analyst of stories – not even Aristotle.

Chapter 1 describes seven elements where professional storytellers generally agree on the basics. In Chapter 2, I cover storytelling structure, in Chapter 3, the intensity curve (what I call 'temperature'), Chapter 4, the ways to design a story, Chapter 5, important details to consider, Chapter 6, the importance of rewriting (mostly ripping out what needs to go), and finally, Chapter 7, how all of this applies to storytelling in games.

Chapter 1

Seven Elements of Storytelling

1.1. A central premise.

1.2. 3D characters who change over time.

1.3. A confined space, often described as a 'crucible.'

1.4. A protagonist who is on some sort of quest.

1.5. An antagonist standing in the way of the hero.

1.6. Everything is getting better or worse – an 'arc.'

1.7. Conflict between the protagonist and antagonist.

1.1. THE CENTRAL PREMISE

The premise is the point of the story, like 'power corrupts,' or 'bad people can be turned to good,' or 'saving the world is worth the effort,' or even things that may not be true in the real world like "good is the same as evil." By the time the audience reaches the end of the story, they should clearly see this point and believe that it is true according to the events of the story. In fact, at its most basic level, the entire story is nothing more than an elaborate set of circumstances built to convince the audience about the premise. Every system with rules has an *objective*, and proving a premise is the objective of storytelling.

To illustrate this in action, imagine a story that tries to say that "good triumphs over evil," yet shows evil people getting off without a penalty all the way to the end. At best, this will feel wrong, and more likely, downright stupid. How would you feel if the Empire won at the end of the original three Star Wars movies? If your point is to say that good triumphs over evil, then in no uncertain terms, good must triumph in the end.

Many stories focus on a binary pair of premise points, for example: 'Power corrupts, but good can redeem the corrupted.' In fact, at the conclusion of the three original Star Wars movies, this combination produces a far more satisfying resolution than the death of Darth Vader alone. Winning a fight would have produced a defeated bad guy, whereas turning Vader to good ended the evil of his life.

Just like the central premise of the story, the main characters have their own personal premises – mainly in the form of what they believe about themselves, even if not entirely true. Personal premises underlay each character's opinions, convictions, and wants. To keep this straight, character premises can be summarized with a simple statement such as 'hard work is important,' or 'I always tell the truth.'

If a character violates a personal premise – for example, a hard-worker who suddenly slacks off, or a truth-teller who tells a self-serving lie – the audience will feel that something is wrong. Their actions are not matching the stories they've been telling about themselves, and unless we are trying to show how a character is self-deceived, it's usually considered a contrivance when a character abandons a personal premise in favor of actions that contradict it.

Characters coming to grips with the central premise of a story drives every part of your tale, and for this reason, the topic rises to the surface in all seven chapters of this book.

1.2. CHARACTERS

The main characters are the people that our audience will come to care about, root for, despise, or even hate. We usually introduce our main characters early in the story. Occasionally, they arrive later. No matter when the audience first encounters a significant character, we need to produce an unambiguous scene that immediately reveals a character's personal premise. The audience needs to know what each character values most, and from this, why anyone might care about them (or choose to dislike them).

It is *critical* to reveal something concrete about our characters right from the get-go. Otherwise, if our audience doesn't see our main characters as someone special and unique and believable and interesting, they won't care what happens to these people later in our story.

The initial character introductions need not be a soup-to-nuts revelation (lots immediately below and also in Chapter 4 on the topic of *'character development')*. There will be plenty of chances to reveal our characters in greater detail while the story progresses. In fact, revealing our characters through their actions will occupy a large portion of our story.

3D, 2D, and 1D characters

Much has been written about differences between '3D' characters, '2D' stereotypes, and one-dimensional wallflowers. This is related to how much each character contributes to the story. Typically, 3D characters include the protagonist, and sometimes one or two close associates. 3D characters also include the antagonist, and sometimes an immediate underling. As much as time and space allow, 3D characters are fully explored.

Upper-level associates and underlings are more often 2D stereotypes. Yet if they are actively involved in planning and execution, they can be developed into 3D characters. Lesser associates and minor henchmen are almost always 2D stereotypes. After their initial intro– ductions, they normally do not evolve.

One-dimensional 'wall-flower' characters aren't 'characters' at all, and they merely float around to keep the place from feeling too empty.

In general, we don't have enough room to fully develop more than a few 3D characters, and we leave lesser characters behind as soon as they are no longer needed. If we drag a 2D character through the whole story, he or she may begin to look like a main character, and this will confuse the audience and slow the whole story down. If you need the same 2D characters from time-to-time, find a reason to store them for later use. A character with a personal-service vocation makes a terrific 2D character, like a car mechanic, baker, or bartender, because each is associated with a place, and they have a reason to stay put.

In short, only *important* characters do *important* things.

What is this thing we call 'character development?'

While a story progresses, the audience continues to learn about the main characters from what they do, and to a lesser extent, what they say and don't say. Through their actions, choices, arguments, and mistakes, a rising pool of evidence reveals each main character's personal premise, genuine personality, strengths, weaknesses, and prefer– ences. Each time our audience sees a new trait or the evolution of a trait over time – *this* is what storytellers call 'character development.' (see Section 1.6. below: *'Arcs'* for more on this).

With added information, the audience will cultivate a growing emotional investment in our main characters, and they will increasingly care about what happens to them. And just like how we come to expect certain behaviors from people in real life, the audience will either root for these characters to succeed or hope they fail.

Conveying a sense of our main characters to the audience is perhaps the hardest part of creative writing. An audience learns about each character based on how the characters are behaving in response to the events of the story, and there is no way around this fact.

We may want in the worst way to have our main characters stand on a soapbox and tell the world about themselves. It would be *so much easier*. But how many people in the real world do that? How many people say what they are really thinking? Real-life characters rarely announce anything about themselves, and to avoid a sickening contrivance, we need to avoid this.

Some writers say f*** it, and have their characters speak directly to the reader, or to the theater audience, or to the game player in the same way a movie actor might communicate with a director between takes. This is called 'breaking the 4^(th) wall,' and it is nothing less than a train wreck because the 'characters' are suddenly nothing more than stage-actors or movie-actors or voice-actors – and no longer 'characters' at all. Like dropping a nuclear bomb on your story, it's the last bomb you will ever drop.

Don't do it.

Any sort of one-way monolog like a soliloquy (speaking as though no one else is there) can become an uninspiring drag because it launches details out of the blue. A monologue is no substitute for character interactions during difficult events, and a one-way dialogue will drain the life from your story. and put your audience to sleep.

Even ordinary dialogue can be draining if not in response to ongoing events in the story. Rootless dialogue is like a college lecture or assigned reading. It can add information, but it is not the same as 'hands-on' learning. In short, if a character says anything at all, it must be in reaction to the events of the story.

As hard as it may be, we need to let our characters react according to who they are – quietly, aggressively, thoughtfully, decisively, deviously, or however else seems to be their proper reaction based on what is happening. As long as our characters behave during intense moments according to their underlying personal premises, they will authentically reveal and reinforce details about themselves. In fact, for most writers, our characters gradually take on a life of their own, and eventually, they refuse to do or say anything 'out of character.'

The same as everyone in the real world, the deepest essence of a character's innermost nature may lay hidden under a veneer of secondary traits. While our story forces a character into new situations, during moments of emotional intensity, these veneers are peeled away, and when this happens, everyone sees the character with greater clarity – including the characters in the story – *especially* the characters in the story.

Characters only *reveal* their innermost essence when compelled by events to *rely* on their innermost essence and this is how we reveal them to the audience.

Here are some parting thoughts on the topic of characters...

■ Our main characters should be larger than life. Nobody in the audience wants to see a story about average people. Average people are boring, and they should never wind up the subject of a story unless they are merely starting out this way, and will rapidly grow from there. When we first meet Luke Skywalker, he's a whiny kid until his past catches up with him and he's forced onto the path of becoming who he was always meant to be, a Jedi knight. Had Luke stayed a whiny kid for much longer, the audience would have hurled and left the movie theater in disgust.

■ The audience must see our main characters as distinct and unforgettable, yet human all the same – even if the story is about an ogre, a donkey, and a fox. No matter how alien or strange our characters may be, *stories are always about human nature,* and our main characters must remain fundamentally human in how they process and react to situations. And this is also true for 2D characters and wall-flowers.

■ Dialog is no substitute for action, and when dialog happens, it should confirm what the audience suspects from the events of the story. Princess Leah could have spewed forever over her love for Han Solo. Instead, she stuck her neck out to rescue him at the beginning of *Return of the Jedi* – and *that* is how we know that her love is genuine.

■ At any given point, the main characters should barely have the strength to take on the next step of their quest. Characters that are too strong never convince the audience that they're up against any real challenges. And this is true for both the main hero and the chief 'bad guy.'

■ Authentic characters grow for obvious reasons – usually based on a peril survived or a loss suffered. Nobody grows in any significant way without extreme circumstances.

■ Main characters should have an extensive life history. Although backstories are mostly known only to the storyteller, these events can also leak into the written story to justify why a character exhibits certain behaviors, especially extremely unexpected or evil actions.

■ Characters should have some weakness that threatens to derail them on their quest. Even Superman, the most overblown and completely unbelievable hero of all time has his problem with kryptonite.

1.3. THE CRUCIBLE

The premise answers the question of what the story is about. The crucible compresses the size of the story and allows the temperature to vary (see Chapter 3: *'The Temperature of the Story'*). A story that wanders around the Universe or unfolds into unrelated circumstances will diffuse the attention of our audience, and this will never compress events enough to produce useful intensity. A story can only produce heat when events are contained within limited boundaries of time and space. For a story to make sense, it must be confined to an interrelated time and place, sometimes called a setting.

Imagine if the Star Wars movies included hours of documentary footage about minor alien species living on nearby planets. Perhaps it might be argued that this information would add useful context. Yet extraneous details are nothing more than pointless distractions. With so many unrelated moving parts, the audience can no longer distinguish what is important from what is mere window dressing (if they haven't already passed out in their seats from relentless boredom).

A sailing ship, a small town, an ethnic neighborhood, an island, a space station – these sorts of places work well because they offer natural boundaries. Why is the story happening here? Why are these particular characters showing up? What's so special about this time, this location, and the events that seem to be taking place here? Answers to those questions help to concentrate the impact and meaning of events and exclude extraneous noise.

Epic stories happen to a lot of characters across many interrelated settings. Simple stories typically happen to a handful of people in just one place. The size of your crucible is not as important as how there must be a crucible, a clearly obvious limitation on where and when the action takes place.

At its time of production, the epic movie, Heaven's Gate was the most expensive fiasco in Hollywood history. There were lots of reasons for this, but many reviewers point to how it was filmed in a random assemblage of disconnected settings. At the other extreme, most of *Apollo 13* was produced inside a practically claustro–phobic setting the size of two utility closets connected nose-to-nose. In comparison to the enormous emptiness of space, the Apollo vehicles compressed the vast danger into an inescapable world unto itself. Most events on Earth were shown inside a single house and a few rooms at Mission Control – and this compressed the desperate effort to bring the astronauts safely home.

When in doubt, shrink the size of your setting, limit the time of events, and reduce the number of characters involved. By compressing the size of your story, you'll have greater freedom to concentrate the action at any point, letting you crank up the heat when you need it most.

1.4. THE PROTAGONIST

The protagonist is the character who carries the audience through the story – our surrogate, our eyes and ears, the character who suffers and succeeds on our behalf. In the parlance of video games, the protagonist is an *avatar* – a gateway for the audience to experience the story nearly firsthand.

While the hero struggles against opposition from all directions, through the magic of our human storytelling hardwiring, the struggle opens our eyes and places us bodily into the story. This is what we call an immersive experience. While the protagonist presses ahead, the audience experiences the same fear, dread, relief, and satisfaction along the way – as though this were our own quest.

This only works because of an odd quirk of our human storytelling hardwiring. Somehow, we can empathize with an external character to the point where we *become the character* – and because the protagonist operates at the center of the story and functions as a doorway to the immersive experience – *the protagonist is the most important character.*

Traditionally, the protagonist is the main good guy character, but not always good in an absolute sense. In fact, we may not even find him to be particularly endearing at all, such as Harrison Ford's character in *Blade Runner*, almost always dark and brooding. But we root for him anyway, because if nothing else, he's the most likable person in the film.

To properly fulfill the role of our personal avatar, the protagonist must see more clearly, understand events sooner, make the better guesses more often, and press ahead when everyone else is ready to jump ship.

Sometimes the protagonist is astounding by merely doing what is sensible in the face of extreme circumstances. For example, in *Schindler's List*, the factory owner is hardly a saint, but in view of how he has chosen to resist the Nazis, he is someone worth caring about.

Here are key points to consider when creating and developing your protagonist...

■ Our audience will only root for someone who is willing to work for success, and they will strongly gravitate toward a protagonist actively pursuing a critically important goal or quest.

■ The protagonist has the best reason to seek the object of the quest and wants to succeed more than anyone else in the story.

■ The protagonist works the hardest, risks the most, and often suffers more than anyone else in the process.

■ The protagonist starts out mostly ignorant of what lies ahead and must learn and grow in order to succeed (see Section 1.6. below: *'Arcs')*.

■ Sometimes the 'protagonist' is a group of like-minded people all working toward a common goal, but this rarely works as well as a central main hero supported with lesser characters. Even if the story includes an ensemble of equals, it is best to clearly single out someone as the lead character.

■ The most believable protagonists always have problems and flaws that constantly gnaw at them. The battle is often against the demons within as much as the hurdles ahead.

■ The protagonist overcomes and defeats the antagonist in a way that proves our premise (see Chapter 4, Section 4.2. for more on proving the premise).

1.5. THE ANTAGONIST

In the same way that we produce a fully-developed protagonist, we also need to reveal an equally-developed, formidable, and believable antagonist. Although an anta—gonist may not see it this way, the antagonist has one job and one job only – to actively and effectively oppose the protagonist.

The protagonist cannot win, and the story cannot end, until the protagonist defeats the antagonist in a proper and fitting way (a way that pulls the essential facts of the story together like the final piece of a jigsaw puzzle, and conclusively demonstrates the point of the premise). Ideally, the antagonist and protagonist are clearly aware of each other's plans, both understand their own *personal* stakes, and both see how there must be a final showdown. One will win, and one will lose. There will be no stalemate, no walking away from the inevitable collision.

A flesh and blood 'bad guy' is by far the most obvious sort of antagonist. Yet an 'antagonist' might be a part of the protagonist's own personality, such as painful memories holding him back. Terrible external circum—stances can act as an antagonist, such as the experience of the Apollo 13 crew after their oxygen tank explosion. The antagonist might be a computer programmed with a human personality like Hal in *2001: A Space Odyssey*.

The antagonist might even be personified weather experienced in a terrible way, as in the movie *The Perfect Storm.*

An antagonist can take any form as long as a sense of conflict between the protagonist and antagonist is engaged and felt on a personal level. Nonetheless, as the antagonist becomes increasingly more abstract, the personal nature of the conflict is harder to show. For example, a grizzly bear can look the protagonist straight in the eye and physically impede his or her progress as a clear matter of choice, whereas an exploding oxygen tank has no conscious malice and there is no interpersonal conflict. When the antagonist is a terrible set of circum—stances, there is work to do. To generate a proper sense of conflict, the protagonist must struggle to engage a faceless enemy. As long as the protagonist genuinely feels obstructed on a deeply personal and emotional level, and as long as there is a solid reason for the protagonist to feel this obstruction in *human* terms, the audience will accept a plausible conflict between the protagonist and antagonist, even if the antagonist isn't human at all.

Rather than a purely evil 'bad guy,' like The Wicked Witch of the West in the *Wizard of Oz*, an antagonist is much more compelling and believable when his goal is directly threatened by the goal of the protagonist. Now, the antagonist has a reason to fight. It's this sort of opposition to the protagonist that really matters, not so much that our antagonist is genuinely evil.

The antagonist's opposition to the protagonist can't be an accident. There must be a conscious choice that produces the conflict. For example, in the movie, *The Perfect Storm*, there is no human antagonist. The captain needs to make a living and decides to head out to sea. The sea is the sea, and it does what it does. Yet there is *still* a reason why the boat encounters the storm. The captain made a choice to ignore obvious warnings.

In the movie *Jason Bourne*, the antagonist is broken into three characters – the CIA chief, the 'Asset,' and the female assistant – all who have their own reasons to oppose the protagonist – one a matter of saving the institution, one a matter of personal revenge, and the other a veiled hope for redemption. Such a fractured assemblage of motivations would be a bad idea for the design of our hero – the *protagonist*. Typically, the audience prefers to root for one individual with a single objective. Yet this sort of unified personality is less important in the design of an *antagonist*, and splitting the antagonist across several characters can produce complex motivations and a nettlesome shifting tide of obstacles.

Ideally, both the protagonist and antagonist attempt to defeat the other based on legitimate, unavoidable, and deeply emotional motivations – and for this reason, I prefer a *single* protagonist and a *single* antagonist. The conflict remains better focused and contained, and there is less to explain. As an example, the emperor is deeply offended when Luke Skywalker rebuffs his final offer to join him on the dark side of the force, whereas Luke is offended when the emperor laughs at Luke's goal to turn Vader away from evil. The climactic scene is not just a battle for control of the galaxy or even a classic fight between good and evil. The battle at the conclusion of *Return of the Jedi* becomes *acutely personal,* and defeating the emperor will settle the practical conflict *and* the emotional score – all in one great face-to-face stroke.

Critically, the protagonist and antagonist must be closely matched in their ability to defeat the other. If the antagonist is too strong – and loses anyway – the protagonist's success is absurd, as we see in the first *Independence Day* movie where immensely powerful aliens fail to conquer the Earth. On the other hand, if the antagonist is too weak, we have no reason to root for the hero.

Here are key points to consider when creating and developing your antagonist...

■ Just like the protagonist, the antagonist grows as the story progresses.
■ Make your antagonist only as 'evil' or 'bad' or 'corrupt' as you need for your story to work. A complicated anta–gonist with many layers of negative and positive attributes is far more believable and engaging than a cookie-cutter 'bad guy.'
■ Ideally, the goals of the protagonist and antagonist lead to an unavoidable and mutually exclusive conflict. As a result, the protagonist and antagonist are standing in each other's way. The antagonist must therefore seek to defeat

the protagonist every bit as much as the protagonist must seek to defeat the antagonist.

■ The antagonist is motivated for a reason, and the audience will be far more convinced about the goals of the antagonist once they see what is driving him.

■ In the same way that the protagonist is encumbered by a thorn in his side that holds him back, the antagonist should have a soft spot or 'humane' side – a human frailty, weakness, or gentler aspect that gnaws away at his com–mitment to 'the plan.'

■ Win or lose, the antagonist must suffer as a consequence of his plan and stand to lose everything if the protagonist wins.

■ The power of the antagonist to resist the protagonist must grow at the same rate as the power of the protagonist to defeat the antagonist – and this growth cannot be a simple 'level up' bonus. An antagonist grows stronger for a reason – just like everyone else in the story.

■ By the end of the story, your audience should wind up learning nearly as much about your antagonist as your protagonist.

1.6. ARCS

For a story to fully satisfy the audience, everything and everyone in the story must change from 'pole to pole,' as they say in the biz. If the protagonist starts out polished and snooty, he must end up grubby and humble. If he starts out a drunk, he must end up sober. If he's angry at the beginning, he must wind up a 'Mr. Nice Guy.' If he is physically strong at first, in the end he must wind up hardly able to walk. And the same sort of change must happen to the setting and every other element and character in the story.

Nothing implies progress more clearly than change. The weather must be getting colder or rainier or darker. The sound must become louder or softer or more sinister. The phases of the Moon must progress. The snow gets deeper. The protagonist faces ever harder challenges. The plans of the antagonist become more complex and insurmountable.

Change from one extreme to the other in a story is often called 'the arc' of the story. Notionally, it is the shape of a continuous line drawn from the North Pole to the South Pole. In *Apollo 13*, the Earth keeps looming larger while time is running out. In *Gone with the Wind,* the mansions of the South fall into disrepair, and with all the slaves gone, the plantation owners are planting their own vegetables.

The weak-minded are getting smarter. The wise are becoming stupid. The unlucky catch a break. Rampant evil is brought to justice.

Nothing stays the same.

1.7. CONFLICT

Characters tend to reveal more about themselves when they are engaged in some sort of strong interpersonal disagreement – an important concept to keep in mind. However, 'conflict' is a far more basic story element than two characters having an argument. All conflict in our story must be rooted in how the protagonist and the antagonist are impeding each other. The protagonist and the antagonist both have critically essential goals, and both are standing in each other's way. This is the underlying central conflict that drives the entire tension of the story. Every conflict we see in every scene ultimately stems directly from the central conflict.

For example, in *The Perfect Storm,* two fishermen are at each other's throats for most of the voyage. The conflict is personal, yet it's fundamentally based on the anxiety of life aboard a small fishing boat far at sea. Their tension boils over and manifests itself in fights of one sort or another, yet the source of their belligerence is derived from the danger all around (the antagonist of the story). The enemy is unspoken, but no mystery.

Suddenly, one of two fishermen is snagged overboard, and his arch-nemesis is the first into the water to save him. These two long-liners may hate each other, but when push comes to shove, we see how much a Gloucesterman will stick his neck out to save another Gloucesterman. The crew knows how the *ocean* is their true adversary, and they won't survive their immediate and fundamental conflict unless they watch each other's backs.

Conflict reveals important aspects of our characters. It reveals their greatest fears, and it shows us how they see the world around them. In moments of interpersonal conflict, people are likely to say just about anything, including huge lies, the naked truth, and a whole lot of other things they might not want others to think about later. If you need a character to say something important, throw them into an interpersonal conflict.

Nonetheless, keep in mind as discussed in Chapter 6, actions always speak louder than words, and what is said should only confirm what the audience already suspects based on previous events.

Next Up: The Structure of the Story

Chapter 2

The Structure of the Story

Beginning, middle, and end

Aristotle had a lot to say about structure in stories. In a nutshell, it comes down to this: Stories should have a beginning, middle, and end. Of course, what we create in each section, and how these sections are used to build the story requires a little more development. And so, as Aristotle advises, I will start at the beginning...

2.1. THE PROLOGUE

As a novel reader, movie audience member, or video game player – we've just paid our 12, 20, or 50 bucks – and before us lies the unknown. We may have heard something about the story ...enough to pique our interest. The book cover artwork, a title screen, a description at our favorite gaming or video streaming site, a Facebook trailer – these are teasers designed to sell the product, not to tell us much about the characters and their story. Even if someone were to sketch the entire plotline for us, we have yet to experience the story for ourselves.

On the other hand, as a new writer, I knew my story inside, and out and I would fret over dropping too many clues in my prologue. I thought that stories were secrets to reveal bit by bit – and if I wasn't careful, too many clues might let the movie audience, or the novel reader, or the game player see right through the entire story, and they'd have no reason to continue. I simply did not want to 'spill the beans' before the story was out of the gate.

But an odd thing happened on my way to becoming a fiction-writer... I discovered that I can't *possibly* drop too many clues in the first scene – the prologue (or just about anywhere else). As a general rule, the audience has no idea what anything means until they see it happen in the context of the story. Excised from the story, a rootless detail tells us nothing about what is happening and what it means. A storyteller could present the entire concluding scene as a prologue (like we see in many stories), and no one would see a single bean out of place.

As it turns out, suspense isn't produced by keeping our audience in the dark. Suspense is produced by revealing as much about our story as fast as we can feed it to the audience. We are not spilling the beans. We are educating our audience ...telling them about the possibilities ...telling them about the world they have entered ...the characters and the problems they face ...what might happen next. It's like learning the rules of a game. Clues tell us what *might* take place, yet nothing about what *will* take place.

In the prologue (Act 1, Scene 1), we school our audience with a *miniature version of the entire story* – showing what will happen, a sense for why it will happen, and the sorts of people who will be in the middle of the action. The audience will not grasp the deeper meaning, but the seeds have been planted, and an intuitive sense of the story has been set in motion.

The prologue may tell a tiny version of the actual story, or a parallel version using metaphorical analogies and symbols. Either way, our brief introductory prologue is *critical* to advancing the story because it points the audience in the right direction, answers all sorts of general questions, and gets the story rolling with a head of steam.

As an example, the introductory scene in the movie *Men in Black* follows the fate of a meandering dragonfly while it drifts through various desert perils. At the end of the prologue, the dragonfly is squashed on the windshield of a vanload of Mexican migrant workers. Perfecto! That is exactly what happens in the rest of the movie – a space alien 'bug' wanders around metropolitan New York City avoiding one peril after another (mainly being chased by the protagonists) …until it winds up squashed in the end. Whether the audience realizes this or not, during the two-minute prologue, they just saw the core elements of the story in a nutshell.

Does the audience feel cheated because the essence of the movie has been laid at their feet? Are they upset that nearly every bean has been spilled? Are they outraged and ready to storm from the movie theater, or demand a pay-per-view refund? Quite the opposite. Suddenly, the audience has a snapshot of the entire story, and they are anxious to learn more about what the prologue means. Of course, they still have no clear idea about what will happen, but they have a *basic* idea. And that is where we need to start.

No matter how baldly obvious the dots connect, until the audience sees the events of our story played out, we have not spilled any beans (for details, see Chapter 5:

'Foreshadowing'). In the original *Planet of the Apes* movie, the astronauts have plainly returned to Earth. Rather than hiding this fact, by planting a host of obvious clues, the audience begins to ignore what must be plainly true, and this produces one of the most powerfully revealing endings in movie history. The audience has every reason to believe that the Planet of the Apes is an odd version of Earth, but until the very end, we do not see how this might be possible.

In fact, a story can begin with the final climactic moment. The movie *Gandhi* starts this way. But rather than spoiling the movie, the opening scene of *Gandhi* convinces the audience that Gandhi, the character, is going to get himself shot over something he did or represents, and the movie will be about this *'something.'*

If there is no sensible way to portray your prologue with a metaphor – like a squashed dragonfly – consider pulling elements directly from your story. No matter what, as long as your prologue delivers a basic story outline, you can borrow any scene from any point.

During the prologue, don't hold back. Tell your audience what the story is about. Once they have a sense for where they are headed, they will settle in for the ride.

2.2. THE SPLASH

If the prologue (Act 1, Scene 1) doesn't state our premise, we must reveal our premise in no uncertain terms in Scene 2. In *Men in Black,* as soon as the dragonfly is smashed on the windshield, we immediately see that aliens are living on Earth – and not just the regular sort of migrant aliens the U.S. government chases through the desert and blocks with inconvenient barriers – but the kind of aliens that come from outer space.

Act 1, Scene 2 – there it is – right in our face with no dithering on the point: Space aliens really do exist, they live among us, and because size doesn't matter, they fit right in. This is the premise of *Men in Black*. Or to put this another way: Claims about space aliens we see on the covers of tabloid newspapers are entirely accurate.

While Scene 2 develops, the point is driven home in every way possible. Nothing is wasted. Even the meta–phor of migrant 'alien' workers comes into play when the smuggler's van from the prologue is discovered by the U.S. border patrol. One of the Mexican 'aliens' hiding in the van is a space alien in disguise, and once the space creature is smeared all over the desert by a Men in Black team, there is no lingering doubt about where the movie is headed. Aliens live on Earth, and agents in black suits work to keep them in line.

Is what the tabloids say about aliens true? It's starting to look that way. Of course, we haven't encountered any tabloid newspapers in the movie, so this exact connection will come later. Yet the Scene 2 splash has made its point, and now it's time for a proper introduction of the main characters – the MiB team we will follow, and a 'bug' on a quest to threaten a galaxy.

2.3. NAILING THE MAIN CHARACTERS

Early in the story, we saw 'K' in a super-tense situation performing with zero anxiety. In fact, we might have noticed that he's about as cool as they come …maybe a bit cooler than he would like to be. Also from this scene, we learn that K's job involves challenging aliens who violate the terms of their Earth visas, and based on the performance of K's elderly partner, it might make sense that K is working to find a younger partner.

In the very next scene, enter James – soon to be 'J.'

We first meet James chasing someone on foot. He's a young fast-running fast-talking New York City cop, but his target is not just fast – he can jump from street-level to the rooftop of a five-story building! Nonetheless, James runs him down the old-fashion human way – finally cornering what is clearly an alien disguised as a human.

Are we convinced that James is an amazing person? Yes. Is he resourceful? Absolutely! Is he funny? That too, especially when he jumps from a bridge onto a moving open-topped tour bus with the excuse of how it's "raining black people all over New York City!"

In less than two minutes, we already have a strong sense of this guy's inner strength, determination, and thorough incapacity to give up.

In a no less memorable way, without skipping a beat, 'Edgar' confronts the bug in the next scene. The bug's spaceship crash-lands into Edgar's pickup truck, and when Edgar, shotgun in hand, swaggers out to investigate, the bug steals his skin. Although the bug's character could have started after it transformed into its own version of Edgar – the *original* Edgar is nearly as irritating and conceited as the space bug – and not a moment is lost in revealing the bug's personality.

In less than 15 minutes, we have a clear picture of the premise, the conflict, and the main characters. 'Act 1' is complete – and the meat of the story can begin.

2.4. THE MEAT OF THE STORY

The middle part of the story is almost always the hardest part to write. We've established the basic setting and circumstances. We have revealed our premise. We have a snapshot of our main characters. Now what?

The answer? We initiate conflict between the protagonist and antagonist, and bring them into closer proximity to intensify this conflict. The protagonist and antagonist each have a primary goal, and as soon as each character is revealed, we reveal what they have in mind – what they are trying to accomplish. In *Men in Black,* the bug wants to steal something called the 'galaxy,' and MiB wants to find out what this is and why the bug wants to steal it. Later, when MiB recognizes the significance of the bug's objective, they will choose to stand in its way.

At first, J and K encounter a crater in Edgar's front yard made by the bug's spaceship. The spaceship is gone, along with the bug in its 'Edgar' suit. The arrival of the bug is a mystery to MiB, but not to the aliens living on Earth. They are leaving in droves. Something is up, a major war perhaps. Meanwhile, the fact that aliens are leaving reinforces the premise of the story at every step – Aliens are on Earth – because otherwise, they would not be leaving!

By sneaking out of Manhattan to reach their various jump-off points, the aliens violate the terms of their visas, and this draws the attention of the entire MiB organ– ization. The aliens know something that MiB hasn't figured out yet – the Earth is about to be blown to bits. Isn't this what supermarket tabloids predict all the time? …the Earth is about to be destroyed by a bunch of pissed- off aliens?

The point is reinforced when aliens working at MiB headquarters quit their jobs and head for the exits. Finally, after a series of gags suggesting a rapidly deteriorating situation, the premise is laid at our feet in no uncertain terms… K consults a tabloid headline, and to the utter amazement of J, he deadpans his verdict: "The most authoritative reporting on the planet."

That's when I fell out of my chair laughing. The tabloids are right. Space aliens exist. The Earth is saved from an alien doomsday on a regular basis. Even Silvester Stallone is an alien!

But now what?

As I write in Chapter 1, the story cannot end until the protagonist defeats the antagonist in a fitting way.

2.5. THE PAYOFF

Throughout the middle of the story, the protagonist (both K and J) come into greater contact with the antagonist (the bug). In each sequence of scenes, the bug comes closer to its quest of stealing the 'galaxy,' and K and J are closer to stopping him. Finally, the bug grabs the galaxy, takes off in a spaceship disguised as a 1964 World's Fair sculpture – and K and J immediately shoot the spacecraft out of the sky.

The bug is furious, so furious that he sheds his Edgar skin, and for the first time we see the thing for what it really is – a 20-foot monster (remember, size does not matter), and now the fight is on to keep the bug from climbing aboard a second spaceship, with K and two blaster weapons in its stomach.

J shows relentless determination when fighting the bug on his own – the same as when we first met him ...and many times since. Originally, J's tenacity was presented as a clue for how the story might play out. Now, it is an essential factor in defeating the bug. With K still inside the bug, and without any useful weapons, J confronts the beast with useless sticks and lots of mouth – surviving the bug's punishing attacks just long enough for K to cut his way out. If not for the first scene where James chases the amazing alien on foot, we might never accept this climactic scene. But we totally accept J's resilience and guts, and based on his fearless persistence, the story drives to its conclusion.

Is there any doubt that the tabloids are right about aliens? Nope! Does the bug wind up squashed – just like the dragonfly we saw squashed during the prologue? Yup! Has the world been saved from space aliens? Most certainly. Has the premise been proven? Without a doubt.

The story is over, and now it's time to roll the credits and send the audience on their way.

2.6. EPILOGUE

The storyteller has produced a satisfying conclusion. The story is over. But sometimes there's a burning question that deserves a brief answer. In *Men in Black*, the movie ends with K retiring and J taking on a new partner. In this case, the epilogue is more of a commercial pitch for the next movie in the series.

Nobody expects a story to wrap up every loose end, and nothing major should happen in an epilogue. At most, we might tie up a pressing question that did not fit the flow of the story. For example, in the MiB epilogue, we see that an agent can be a woman …a reasonable question to address. If you decide on an epilogue, keep it short, and if possible, leave it out altogether.

You may have noticed I'm using the same story–telling structure in this chapter. Below, I conclude with my own epilogue …potentially distracting points had I raised them in the main body of the text…

Additional points to consider on the topic of story structure...

■ As much as possible, use foreshadowing to plant as many clues about what happens next as time and space allow (see Chapter 5 for more on this). For example, K tells J to "never press the 'red button' unless I tell you to." Obviously, K will ask J to press this button. If we hadn't been told about the red button, and how it is only for a special purpose, we would have missed the emotional payoff when the time comes to press it.

■ The crucible for this story is the New York City metropolitan area (space aliens are confined to New York City because no one will notice they are there). The story is also bounded by the Archelien ultimatum to return the galaxy within one galactic week (one hour). Based on these boundaries, the story cannot wander very far geographically, or continue indefinitely.

■ Notice the arcing. The orderly MiB headquarters gets trashed. Who among the main characters is left unchanged? The bug transforms from something resem-bling a bumbling human to a menacing 20-foot monster. K finally gets his dream to quit. The pathologist who starts out saying that she hates the living becomes much more engaging in her demeanor. Edgar's wife has her life back. J gradually gets a handle on this 'alien thin,' and eventually earns the respect of the big boss, Zed. Even the Earth-like Unisphere sculpture is flattened! And that damned bug finally gets squashed!

■ Just like we read in the tabloids, the real Earth – the one we never realized was in constant danger – has been saved. And beyond a few MiB agents and a few thousand space aliens, no one takes the threat seriously.

Great story.

Next Up: The Temperature of the Story

Chapter 3
The Temperature of the Story

3.1. Taking the temperature.

3.2. The City on the Edge of Forever.

3.3. The temperature curve.

3.4. The midpoint crisis.

3.5. The beginning of the end.

3.6. The conclusion.

3.7. The end.

3.1. TAKING THE TEMPERATURE

The fundamental nature of storytelling is an emo–tional experience, and inducing a sense of reality involves writing our story to match a deeply anticipated hardwired pattern of emotional peaks and valleys. We do not tell a fictional story to educate our audience. We tell our story to *entertain* them.

Emotional peaks and valleys can be described in terms of the *temperature of the story*. Specifically, the 'temperature' is the intensity of the audience's emotional response at any given moment. In order to draw the audience into an immersive experience, the temperature must rise and fall according to an expected level of emotional intensity at each stage of the story. The temp–erature sends a signal and tells the audience where they are in the story… at the beginning, heading toward the middle, at the middle, heading toward the end, or very near the end. And amazingly, as long as the temperature curve follows the pattern expected by the audience, the events of the story can happen in almost any order within the timeframe and locations of the crucible (see Chapter 1, Section 1.3: *'The Crucible'*).

As mentioned earlier, our experience of a story is rooted in the activities of the protagonist – our emotional avatar. Sometimes, the setting, the music, or a seemingly inconsequential background scene will engender a change in emotional intensity. But this feeling does not come into any sort of sharp focus until the audience sees how the protagonist is reacting to the situation. When the protagonist searches in vain for a lost sacred object, the audience feels the same growing sense of panic. When the protagonist is hopeful about his or her immediate prospects, the audience feels equally relieved. And when our hero decides to go where no one has gone before, the audience embraces this quest as their own.

If we were to chart the emotional temperature on a graph while the story unfolds …plotting a zero when there is no response from the audience, and 100 when their minds are about to blow – we would see a record of ups and downs that correspond to how the story is affec– ting our audience at any given moment along the way.

Some writers chafe at the notion of one particular temperature curve working better than another. But I must caution you, as someone who has learned this the hard way – there is a preferential pattern nonetheless …a pattern built into our human hardwiring via natural selection over the last 250,000 years. If the writer chooses to ignore this pattern in any significant way, the story will likely induce nothing more than pure frustration.

If you want to reach an audience in a way that does not confuse or piss them off – like it or not – your aud– ience will be looking for a specific long-ago-established set of temperature clues. This is how people are built to process a story …whether the story is told inside a computer game, a novel, or the confines of a science fiction television episode.

Now for a truly awesome example…

3.2. THE CITY ON THE EDGE OF FOREVER

First broadcast in 1967, episode 28 of the original *Star Trek* series, *The City on the Edge of Forever,* is perhaps the best-written and directed science fiction television episode of the 20th Century. The story begins with the crew of the Enterprise investigating a planet at the heart of intense time distortions. The distortions periodically convulse the orbiting ship, and during one particularly strong wave, the helmsman is injured, and the ship's doctor is called in. Immediately, with a small injection from Dr. McCoy, Sulu is revived, good as new.

All seems well enough until another wave strikes the ship, causing McCoy to accidentally inject himself with the *entire* remaining contents of his hypo. The doctor freaks out from the effects of the drug, fights his way off the bridge, transports himself to the planet's surface, and arrives at the source of the time disturbance.

Led by Captain Kirk, with support from Science Officer Spock, a landing party transports to the surface in hot pursuit. When they arrive, they discover a planet in ruins – and very old ruins indeed – perhaps as old as 10,000 centuries by Spock's estimate.

While most of the landing party searches for McCoy, Spock, and Kirk take a moment to inspect the ancient relics, particularly an intriguing annulus – the singular source of the time distortions. For at least a million years, this annulus has waited for an opportunity to disclose its nature and purpose...

"I am the Guardian of Forever," it announces, "part machine and part living being" – a time portal able to transport anyone to any time and place in history on any planet.

Without asking, the Guardian demonstrates its power by replaying Earth's past. Transportation is accomplished by passing through the annulus while historical events are rendered. Want to visit ancient Egypt? Wait for an image of ancient Egypt to appear – and be ready to jump.

McCoy is soon discovered, and briefly subdued. But under the intense stimulation of the drug, the crazed doctor quickly awakens, breaks past the startled landing party, and leaps into the time portal just beyond Kirk's wild diving tackle.

He missed him! HE MISSED HIM!!

To deal with this situation, it will take all of their scientific know-how – including the support of their ship, and possibly the brightest minds of the Federation. Yet suddenly, the Enterprise is no longer orbiting overhead. In fact, according to the Guardian, all that they have ever known – their ship, the Federation of Planets, and human space travel *never happened.*

McCoy has somehow altered the past in a big way. The landing party no longer belongs to any time. They are totally out of place ...totally disconnected ...totally on their own.

Kirk decides that he and Spock will travel through the portal. By timing their leap exactly, they hope to arrive in the past before McCoy shows up ...discover how

McCoy might alter the flow of history ...and stop him before this happens. Is this possible? They have little choice but to try. To guide their time of entry, Spock synchronizes his tricorder instrument to the Guardian's replay of human history. Kirk and Spock will leave at the closest possible moment – arriving perhaps a week or a month ahead of McCoy. If they are successful, the Guardian promises to return all three travelers, and everything will be restored to how it was.

Moments before their jump, Kirk issues one final order to those left behind... If Kirk and Spock do not return within a reasonable length of time, the rest of the landing party must enter the portal themselves ...until McCoy is found and stopped ...or the entire party becomes irreversibly trapped to live out the rest of their lives without a past.

Other than dying on a dead planet, there is no other choice.

3.3. THE TEMPERATURE CURVE

Initially, out of pure anticipation, the audience, or reader, or game-player begins with a temperature of roughly 10 on the scale of 0 to 100. During the prologue, the introduction of the premise, and the initial entrance of our main characters, the story should rise to around 50, peaking at this level when the central dilemma or quest is revealed. The early temperature must be high enough to garner audience interest, but still leave room for higher temperatures later in the story. In Episode 28, the initial peak of 50 is the point when Kirk and Spock make their jump into the past.

Having reached this early peak, the protagonist and supporting characters begin a process of adjusting to their practical situation. During this time they discover more about their dilemma and begin to see that nothing about this will be easy. Clearly, there is more to learn before they can achieve their quest. The pace of the story is slow enough now that the storyteller has time to drop a host of preplaced clues and symbols for later use in the story. For the most part, this is our last chance to plant any meaningful hooks, signs, or symbols that we will need later.

Gradually, the temperature meanders down to almost zero, and when the descent finally levels off, this signals the arrival of a critical decision – *the 'midpoint crisis'* – where the protagonist's notional idea of 'what must be done' collides with reality – and now he must commit to the quest whole-heartedly – in full view of what it may cost him (more on this in the next section, 3.4.: *'The Midpoint Crisis')*.

Initially, Kirk and Spock steal contemporary clothes to match their 1930s New York City setting. They also need a place to live, money to pay for this, and extra money so Spock can build a memory circuit to help decipher his tricorder readings (recorded before *and* after McCoy changed the flow of time). And amidst all of this adjustment, they *still* need to find McCoy!

So far, they have no idea how McCoy screws up time or where to look for him. But with each new scene, Kirk and Spock learn a bit more – building toward a crisis that can only be resolved through a major decision. The audience does not see it this way – not yet. They simply see Kirk and Spock working to solve minor problems. Yet like a gathering storm, the pieces are falling into place, and they are preparing for what lies ahead.

Kirk and Spock catch an early break when their new employer – a rescue mission operator named Edith Keeler sets them up with a 'flop' for two dollars a week and gives Kirk a job at 15 cents an hour – hardly enough for room and board much less the 'two kilos' of platinum Spock will need for his electronics project.

Weeks pass. Progress on Spock's memory circuit is painfully slow. McCoy may arrive at any moment. Meanwhile, Kirk is spending time with Edith, and they are growing fonder with each passing day.

Leading up to the midpoint of the story, the scope and difficulty of the quest are becoming apparent, and the protagonist and other characters are developing a deeper understanding of their practical impediments. Minor victories have been won. Yet no significant progress has taken place. The central dilemma is still a notional idea. The protagonist is worried, but hasn't yet come face to face with a critical choice. All of this will change.

The midpoint crisis has arrived.

3.4. THE MIDPOINT CRISIS

In a nutshell, the midpoint crisis is a point of decision …the hardest decision the protagonist will make. The first half of our story includes the prologue, an introduction of the main characters, and a loosely-defined quest where the protagonist gradually learns about the problem he or she is facing. Something needs to be resolved, it is clearly important and worthy of attention, but the details remain unclear. Kirk and Spock have traveled through time to stop McCoy. Frodo and his companions are working their way closer to Mordor. In Men in Black, aliens are leaving Earth, and a bug has shown up. But the basic conflict is still fuzzy. The quest remains ill-defined. What is the protagonist really up against? …its truest extent?

At the midpoint crisis, the enormity of the quest and the cost of success are both fully revealed. No matter how high the cost of success had seemed to this point, the true price of success is suddenly far more personally painful than the protagonist ever imagined. In fact, facing the cost of *success* is now fully entwined with facing the cost of failure. The truth has been revealed, and the protagonist must choose to accept the quest in its most complete form, and facing this choice *is the midpoint crisis.* Until this choice is made, the story cannot advance another inch.

To this point, the quest has focused on discovery. But now, the quest will require a *commitment*. The protagonist finally understands the extent and significance of the antagonist's plans and actions – the widest dimensions of the conflict, and what may be required to win the final battle, to defeat the antagonist and his plans. The cost of doing nothing is terrible, and yet by accepting the quest, the *personal* cost to the protagonist is equally terrible. There is no more time for discovery. The protagonist must choose to accept the quest with all of its personal costs or walk away and suffer the wider consequences.

Our human storytelling hardwiring requires a very specific response... In view of every foreseeable conse–quence, the protagonist must plainly commit to the quest. To do this, as explicitly as possible, the protagonist must answer two central questions... *Will you pursue the quest all the way to its conclusion?* In a vacuum of information, 'yes' would be an easy answer, but the choice also comes with a second question... Knowing how much this may harm you personally, *are you willing to pay any price for success?*

The audience will only believe that a protagonist is absolutely serious and fully committed to the quest when the protagonist also accepts the personal consequences of this choice. By accepting the quest, the protagonist accepts a pathway of personal suffering, and the extent to which the protagonist willingly embraces this mantle defines the extent to which the audience will root for his or her success.

The midpoint crisis concludes when the protagonist takes the first practical step. Now, the second half of the story can begin. Luke Skywalker ends his training and heads for a confrontation with Darth Vader *(The Empire Strikes Back)*. Jim Lovell and his crew power down their command module *(Apollo 13)*. In Episode 28, Kirk accepts that Edith Keeler's life is the key to the future.

The goal of the quest is plain to see. But the quest is still unresolved, and exactly how to proceed remains unclear. To work out the solution in detail, deliberate action is required. The right pathway must be discovered and taken, and the protagonist must use this pathway to defeat the antagonist.

Spock and Kirk see that Edith dies in a routine traffic accident. Minutes later, they see an alternate version where she lives at least six years longer. Spock's electronics burn out before they can learn the meaning of either path. Clearly, Edith is a focal point in time, and whatever McCoy does or does not do with respect to Edith is the key to restoring the future. Perhaps McCoy causes Edith's death and Kirk needs to protect her. Or perhaps McCoy saves Edith, and for the sake of the proper flow of time, Edith must die. What should Kirk do if they find McCoy?

Earlier in the story, for the sake of humanity, his ship, and his crew, Kirk had every reason to assume he'd do what he needed to do. But he never knew what that might entail. At the midpoint crisis of Episode 28, Kirk is tormented by the possibility that the 'right choice' might force him to essentially kill the woman he loves. If Edith must die, he must allow this to happen, and to prepare himself for action when the time comes, he must decide this *now*. He must accept the quest with all of its potential consequences.

As a writer, setting up the midpoint crisis is all about the audience and their commitment to the protagonist. Is the protagonist truly worthy? The audience must see a genuine heartfelt reason to believe this. The authenticity of the protagonist's midpoint crisis decision will drive the audience to root whole-heartedly for success – and not just success in reaching the stated goal, but also success in facing and surviving the enormous emotional cost.

Desperate to learn the answer to Edith's fate, Kirk orders Spock to crack a safe containing a jeweler's tool kit. When Edith discovers how Kirk and Spock borrowed these tools, she threatens to throw them back onto the street. But then she sees how Kirk totally trusts Spock's honesty, and something about her unique capacity for human understanding allows her to accept Spock's promise to return the tools by morning. Even though Kirk does not fully understand, this is his final clue. This is what makes Edith unique, and this is why Edith must die.

The decision at the midpoint crisis must lead to a direct engagement with the antagonist ...whatever its form. Luke must leave his Jedi training to face Vader. Jim Lovell must instruct his crew to abort their mission to the Moon. Kirk must accept whatever Spock's repaired circuit reveals. As insurmountable as the decision may be, there can be only one acceptable choice.

Gene Kranz, Apollo 13's principal flight director famously makes his decision in no uncertain terms... "Gentlemen," he bellows, "*failure is not an option*!" In fact, 'failure is not an option' is the *premise* of the movie, and the midpoint decision is both a commitment on the part of the protagonist to the quest and the point where the audience begins to see what it will take to prove the premise of the story. Gene Kranz is standing on the very tip of the sharpest sword in human history, and he is not going to lose this crew!

When the audience is convinced that our protagonist is fully committed to the success of the quest, the temperature rises to 90 out of 100. But it won't stay there for long.

3.5. THE BEGINNING OF THE END

The story has reached the beginning of the end, and the temperature will now begin a series of downswings and upswings ...each subsequent swing dropping lower and peaking higher.

From the midpoint crisis until the climactic scene of the story, the protagonist will attempt to resolve the conflict in ways that come up short. With each skirmish, the hero will temporarily approach the goal, learn something useful, and often gain a temporary advantage. But this is not enough to succeed, and the protagonist is beaten back by the efforts of the antagonist. Preliminary skirmishes always involve a conflict between the goals of the protagonist and the goals of the antagonist. Prior to the final climactic encounter, there will be at least one skirmish, usually two or three, and never more than a half-dozen skirmishes in all.

Failure may not be an option, but there are always setbacks along the way. During each new attempt to defeat the antagonist, the protagonist will come closer to winning, and *subsequently fail* to a greater extent. Based on this pattern of events, the temperature will peak higher with each new temporary success, and crash deeper with each subsequent failure – maybe from 50 to 30, 60 to 20, 70 to 10, and finally from 80 to zero. During these skirmishes, don't let any peak rise above 80. You'll need to save the highest temperatures for the final climactic encounter.

Between each skirmish, the main characters reaffirm their commitment to the quest (or defeating it). After each skirmish, the next skirmish is harder to face, often leading to conflicts among the protagonist and his team (and often among the 'bad guys').

Meanwhile, the protagonist decides what to do next, and the antagonist prepares for another onslaught. None of the skirmishes have substantially weakened the anta–gonist in any noticeable way. This may not be true ...but this is how the protagonist is seeing the situation. In reality, skirmishes are making things worse for both sides. The protagonist is running short on supplies, and the antagonist is raising more obstacles – and for everyone involved, this consumes valuable resources, and opens unforeseen vulnerabilities.

Nonetheless, there is also a sense that progress is underway. With each skirmish, the protagonist is making inroads and learning more about the antagonist – thereby raising the temperature of the story. Yet with mounting failure and dwindling capabilities, the protagonist is becoming increasingly disheartened, and this sense of defeat is crashing the temperature.

Finally, near the end of the story, the last of these failed engagements leaves the protagonist hanging by a thread, devoid of options, and fully doubting the achievability of the quest. After this final skirmish, the protagonist is finished. Doomed.

There is no hope in sight. He's got no bullets left to shoot. The antagonist is closing in.

The temperature has crashed to zero.

Absolute defeat is standing on the protagonist's doorstep.

In episode 28, Spock finally gets his memory circuit working, and Edith's two possible fates are fully revealed. Edith is a genuinely remarkable woman. In the same way that she is accepting of Spock's borrowed tools, she has an innate ability to convince powerful people to undertake peaceful resolutions to geopolitical conflicts. It is a great gift, but it has arrived at the wrong time in history. In the near future, according to one possible path for her life, she will build a highly effective peace movement at the outset of World War II – thereby delaying American involvement and allowing time for Nazi Germany to build an atomic bomb. Germany wins the war and conquers the world.

Talk about screwing up history!

Spock's tricorder also shows the *second* possibility – the uncorrupted version of history. Sometime over the next few days, Edith will be killed in a pedestrian accident. Evidently, McCoy prevents this accident, and to repair history, no one can intervene – not McCoy – not Kirk.

Kirk is crushed beyond words. Doing nothing will ruin the future, but doing *something* will lead directly to the death of Edith Keeler. Briefly, just briefly, we are left to wonder if Kirk will act when the time comes.

At the end of the story, the protagonist must reaffirm his commitment one last time, and accept the unavoidable consequences. Even a larger-than-life hero like Kirk has his doubts, and in the face of the whole truth he is clearly wavering – and Spock can see this.

Spock's unassailable logic is as simple as it is undeniable… If Edith does not die, the proper flow of time will be lost forever, and to save his ship, his crew, and to restore the future, Kirk must let Edith Keeler die. Time is a cruel master! Time is the enemy!! And in the end, Spock's cold logic will save the future – not love.

Each passing opportunity for an accident fills Kirk with rising agony, and with each false alarm, Kirk fights the same battle in his mind. How can he actively let Edith die? Nevertheless, he has made his choice – the right choice – and now he will pay the price for it. When the time comes, he will stand in McCoy's way.

3.6. THE CONCLUSION

At the end of the story, after a series of increasingly intense setbacks, the protagonist is beaten down and hopeless. The temperature should be sitting at zero. As it turns out, our storytelling hardwiring has been waiting for this zero-temperature signal. A temperature of zero late in the story after a series of partial successes and failures marks the beginning of the conclusion – a 'lull before the storm' that signals the audience to expect the *last battle* – the final engagement that resolves the basic conflict of the story.

At the peak of the concluding sequence, the protagonist dismisses all remaining reservations and plunges ahead without hesitation. In so doing, the protagonist defeats the antagonist and proves the premise in no uncertain terms. This moment in the story is often called the 'fitting conclusion' …the point when the central and final jigsaw piece falls into place, the point where the audience encounters the central meaning of the story in its most complete form. What is the basic conflict of Episode 28? …the proper flow of time versus the cost to set things straight. What is the premise? …the same as many Star Trek episodes – 'The needs of the many outweigh the needs of the few.' What is the final jigsaw piece? …an impossibly high price is paid by the protagonist.

From the very beginning of your story, you have been building toward this moment – every character, every scene, every clue, every minor conflict, every temporary victory, and every failure …all of this driven to a single point. You have reached the moment of resolution where the protagonist will now encapsulate the entire point of the story in a conclusive action.

How is this accomplished?

Just when all hope hits rock bottom, some last tidbit of information, or overlooked resource, or scrap of insig–nificant information comes to light. It was sitting in plain sight – long ago placed and revealed during the prologue and perhaps leaked many times into open view throughout the story as a subtle reminder. Until the climactic scene, no one understood the significance of this 'tidbit.' It could be a tiny hidden weakness in the antagonist, or maybe a 'red button' – at first, a joke that suddenly becomes the only way through a blocked highway tunnel. In Episode 28, Spock's memory module finally reveals the truth. No matter what the tidbit might be, the meaning is simple: The protagonist has one last hope – one last chance for victory. There will be no more chances after this. It is all or nothing, hell or high water, victory or defeat.

Starting with the recognition of the 'tidbit' – and its critical value – the temperature takes off and continues to climb as high as it can go, all the way up to 100 without any more dips along the way until the climactic scene is over. The final sequence has no lulls, no pauses, nothing to prevent a clean and direct engagement between the protagonist and the antagonist. Both bring their A-games to the table. Both have everything to gain and everything to lose.

Until the antagonist is defeated in a fitting way, and the quest has been safely secured, the temperature must not level out for a second. The die has been cast. The final battle is underway. There will be no respite. Everything that matters is teetering in the balance – tilting between success and failure, death and victory, salvation and doom. There will be only one winner, and at the very peak of the final battle, the outcome is fully in doubt.

At the conclusion of Episode 28, a delivery van arrives on the scene. Kirk can see that the truck is heading straight for Edith. He has a brief opportunity to save her, and this is plain to see. But Kirk understands that as soon as Edith dies, the rift in time will be defeated. Kirk will never see Edith again, but he won't save her – nor will he let McCoy intervene. Kirk is committed to his quest. He has *already* made his choice.

The exact details of a climactic sequence do not matter as much as how the tension keeps growing right to the end. It can be a physical battle, or a courtroom scene where the case suddenly turns on a critical piece of evidence, or perhaps a mountain climber who sees an impending storm and must rescue the others before the storm strikes. In some way, the climax of the story is a mad dash to the end where no one pulls their punches. Everything previously placed in the story to this point is available and at our fingertips ready to focus and compress the climactic sequence of events. Luke begins his battle to the death against Vader. The Apollo 13 command module begins to re-enter the Earth's atmosphere on failing batteries and questionable heatshield. Kirk confronts his moment of truth.

When McCoy finally shows up in Episode 28, the story races to its conclusion. At first, McCoy is in a psychotic state, but under the care of Edith, he begins to recover. Eventually, McCoy is able to think and act rationally and he begins to wander around the rescue mission unescorted. Kirk is walking with Edith to a Clark Gable movie when he hears about her new friend, 'Doctor McCoy,' and suddenly Kirk knows he must find McCoy! **NOW!!**

Kirk tells Edith to stay put, and runs across the street where he finds Spock and McCoy standing in the doorway of the rescue mission. In those same moments, Edith waves from across the street completely absorbed by Kirk's sudden transformation, and the strange sight of McCoy rejoicing with familiar faces.

Despite Kirk's warnings, Edith begins to cross the street toward the trio of Federation officers. McCoy sees her walking into the path of the delivery van. She is oblivious to her immediate danger. But before McCoy can take a step, Kirk does not miss his chance this time. Instead of letting McCoy slip through his grasp, he clamps onto the doctor as though he were holding back time itself.

Edith is struck and killed by the delivery van. Time has been set right again, and while the 100-degree story temperature momentarily lingers, the meaning sinks into the eyes of our main characters.

"I could have saved her!! – DO YOU KNOW WHAT YOU JUST DID!!!" Screams McCoy.

"He knows, doctor," says Spock to the night air. Kirk says nothing and instead twists into a brick wall clenching his fists in agony.

"He knows all too well."

3.7. THE END

Upon their success – as promised – the Guardian immediately returns Kirk, Spock, and McCoy to their own time. All is now as it should have been. The Enterprise is in orbit. The Federation of Planets exists as before. From the perspective of the remaining landing party, the three time-travelers arrived just moments after they left. When the story is over – Stop.

Let the temperature drop like a rock, thereby leaving the audience with an internal afterglow. Add nothing new that might distract from this feeling. If at all possible, leave out an epilogue.

The story of Edith Keeler ends faster than any other Star Trek episode. When the Guardian offers the landing party another opportunity to travel through time, using the 'h' word for the very first time on American broadcast television, Kirk ignores the Guardian altogether and simply says to his crew, "Let's get the hell out of here!"

Next Up: Designing the Story

Chapter 4

Designing the Story

4.1. TRUCKERS AND ROAD BUILDERS

The first step in learning to design a story is realizing how the *experience* of a story is not the same as *writing* a story. Anyone who has tried to design a video game already knows this. Playing a game is nothing like building a game for other people. Our skill as a game-player, or book-reader, or movie audience member may offer an eye and ear for what might seem right or wrong in a story – but almost nothing about how to design a story from scratch.

Consuming a story is like the relationship of a long-haul trucker to a highway. The road enables his deliveries, but he understands almost nothing about how the highway was built ...how this particular route was chosen ...how the land was altered ...how bridges and drainage systems were engineered. A truck driver works to deliver a truckload of cargo, and he doesn't care how the road was designed and constructed. He just wants the road to be there.

On the other hand, writing a story is like the work of a civil engineer who considers a host of choices never contemplated by those using the road... Are the bridges high enough for river traffic? ...has she placed enough drainage near desert washes? ...is the paving material suitable for local winter weather? Both our trucker and civil engineer are highway experts of a sort, but the expertise needed to drive atop a finished highway is not the same as the expertise required to design and build a highway.

Reading a book is not the same as writing a book. Watching a movie is not the same as making a movie. To play a game is not the same as designing a game. As a member of the audience, we can usually distinguish the difference between good and bad storytelling, and just like a trucker who notices every bump in the road, we may have all sorts of opinions about plots and character development. But consuming a story does not transform a typical audience member into a storyteller any more than a bumpy road produces a civil engineer. And so, before we go any further, we need to learn how stories are built from the ground up.

4.2. DECIDING WHERE TO GO

A clearly stated goal is the most important factor in any design. In transportation engineering, the goal might focus on selling a flashy sports car with lots of performance, or maybe a truck with a practical amount of cargo capacity. What is the point of a flashy sports car? To draw attention and provide an entertaining driving experience. What is the point of a truck? To haul stuff from point-to-point. What is the goal of our story? To prove our premise.

Proving our premise

The idea of 'proving the premise' is simple: I prove my premise by designing a story that clearly demonstrates how the premise is true. When I begin to outline my story,

I don't start with detailed events, specific characters, cute dialog, massive explosions, robots, or meticulously developed settings. Instead, I focus on what sort of story will help me illustrate my premise, and in the end, thoroughly prove it in a satisfying way.

If my story has the premise: 'Good defeats evil,' my story will focus on good triumphing over evil. In fact, based on this premise, I already suspect I will need a manifestly 'good' protagonist and a clearly 'evil' anta–gonist, and I am beginning to think about situations where 'evil' must be prevented or overturned. Beyond that, I don't know anything. But I've *already* made the most important decision I will make. I have a *goal* that will fundamentally guide all subsequent decisions.

In the same way that the design of a sports car is governed by the goal to create a flashy, drivable, and entertaining automobile – and just like how every com–ponent of a truck is designed to focus on the goal of a practical cargo-hauling vehicle – from this point forward, the components of my story will be selected and assembled with my premise in mind.

How do we demonstrate that our premise is true?

Starting in our prologue, we work to clearly, absolutely, and unambiguously reveal our premise. Immediately after this, and throughout the story, we produce a series of conflicts that can only be resolved if the premise is true. If '*good triumphs over evil*' – then conflicts will center on good fighting evil, and good will succeed in the end. This tells us nothing about what will happen in detail, but it sets a limitation on the sorts of events that might take place and offers a way to filter and select these events when adding scenes to the story.

When I am deciding on what to write, I remind myself about the premise, and use this as a guide to ignore ill-fitting action, irrelevant dialogue, and everything else that does not fit. Anything that distracts from my goal of proving the premise is discarded from my mind, and I instead focus on actions that drive the story in the direction of the final climactic scene. The final climactic scene will seal my case – my goal of 'proving the premise' – and like a court case presenting evidence, everything prior to this point should drive our story in this direction. In the end, the final climactic scene should be the only possible conclusion, and by driving in this direction throughout the story, we are working toward proving our premise.

If the premise is *'The needs of the many outweigh the needs of the few'* – I might set up a situation where lots of people are endangered, then develop circumstances where a single painful sacrifice will be required to save a vast population – a price to be paid by the protagonist. To prove my premise, I will place the protagonist on the horns of an inescapable dilemma, leaving him with just this one choice. It is a real choice – he can run away and let people die, or he can save them at great cost to himself. When he chooses to make his sacrifice, he will prove my premise.

In the end, if I stick to proving my premise, each part of the story will build toward a satisfying conclusion. Like a sports car made from cast aluminum, sheet metal, wiring, plastic, paint, and everything else – when every part is properly assembled according to our goal – we are done.

How do we make this happen in detail?

We define a set of parameters.

4.3. PARAMETERS

A 'premise' is the highest-level definition of our story. Right below this level, we have a set of important questions to answer... Is our story a comedy or a tragedy? What sorts of characters should we include? What kinds of settings might be most suitable? The premise is the central theme holding the entire story together. Parameters set limits on the scale, temperament, and details of your story (see Chapter 1, Section 1.3: *'The Crucible'*). For example, in Episode 28, Kirk and Spock travel to 1930s New York City – an alien and familiar place. In *Apollo 13*, the crew is heading for the Moon aboard a similarly alien and familiar spacecraft.

The written form of a parameter is a 'specification.' For a truck, specifications might focus more on its cargo capacity and heavy-duty structure. For a sports car, specifications might focus more on the user experience, such as cornering ability, or sound system performance. Parameters are not the actual design decisions, but rather objectives and limitations used to guide those decisions.

For a character in a story, a specification might start with something like a 'handsome gentlemen,' which is later used to set limits on the character's physical and emo–tional capacities.

Parameters stem from a clearly-stated premise – and this is where we begin. Here are important questions to consider when working out the parameters of your story:

- What premise do you want to prove?
- Who would you like to see in the story?
- Where would you like the story to happen?
- When would you like this story to take place?
- How do I pull these pieces into a story?

What premise do you want to prove?

As mentioned in Chapter 1, the premise can be any statement of fact, even something untrue in the real world (such as the premise of *Men in Black,* which suggests that aliens are real and the Earth is about to be destroyed). But how do we select our premise in the first place?

In my own writing, I am looking to select a premise that will galvanize and infuse my thoughts, something that is undeniably stimulating to me and genuinely thought-provoking. While sketching and outlining ideas for my story, a theme will emerge. Some of my personal favorites are along the lines of how honorable people stand between civility and tyranny.

Pick something that matters to you, put that thought into words, and stick with it.

A critical part of any premise is how it should include a measure of doubt. The possibility of failure satisfies our audience when the protagonist wins, not the sense of a foregone conclusion. In the movie *Apollo 13*, Gene Krantz declares that "failure is not an option." However, we all can see that failure is a distinct *possibility*. In fact, the possibility of failure drives the tension of every scene. Will the premise survive the events of this story? As long as the audience remains unconvinced about the certainty of a story's outcome, the writer is free to place the protagonist on the horns of a dilemma, free to expose the hero to the possibility of defeat, and free to offer the antagonist a realistic chance to win. We select the words of our premise planning to prove that it is true. But we also need to imagine lots of ways our premise might fail.

Just about every idea for a premise has been explored at one time or another, and trying to cough up something truly unique is unnecessary. Many excellent stories have been written based on fairly ordinary-sounding premises, like 'good will overcome evil,' or 'decency will prevail in the midst of horror.' Pick something that resonates, and don't worry if somebody else has tried to make this point in other stories. Your story can make the same point in an entirely unique way, and no one ever notices or cares if this point has been made before.

If the idea of creating a premise feels foreign to you, you can get a feel for this by stating the premises of stories you have experienced lately. In one brief sentence, write what the story is trying to demonstrate (not a synopsis of what is happening). A well-written story will broadcast its premise in many different ways. Sometimes, a character will state the premise straight out, such as Spock in the second Star Trek movie when declares that "the needs of the many outweigh the needs of the few." Spock has saved the crew and is paying for this act with his life. For the sake of educating the audience, his words are almost unnecessary – we already get it. But where Spock wants everyone to know that he made a conscious choice, not a foolhardy blunder, it is a powerful point in a powerful scene. Spock speaks the words of the premise at the very moment when he has just proven the premise, and we will never forget this moment.

People who speak passionately on a topic often pro–claim a premise word-for-word, sometimes spinning it into a repeating catchphrase, like Martin Luther King's famous "I have a dream" speech in Washington, where the point is how he believes that his dream will one day be a reality.

When I am trying to conjure my own premise, I'll write for a while until I find what I really want to say – then I will work to capture this idea with one simple phrase. Some writers prefer to keep on writing page-after-page until they find a premise. I've done this, and it can work. All the same, an early draft written without a stated premise is usually too much of a mess to salvage, and once I know what I want to say, it's usually best to set early material aside, and start from scratch.

Whatever the method, I know that I will never stop running around in circles until my premise is defined in no uncertain terms. In fact, while rewriting one story, I spent nine years dissatisfied with my premise. In fact, a much better premise was sitting in plain view, and once I put this at the center of my story, I could finally write a satisfying conclusion. No one has time to waste, and getting the premise settled is always worth the effort.

Pick something. Try it on for size. Sketch ideas for characters and settings to help your thoughts, but don't write anything concrete until you've written your premise and taped it to the side of your computer screen. Remember – a premise is the anchor and reference point for every character, setting, idea, and conflict in your story. Work as long as it takes to produce a premise that feels right. Once you know what you want to prove, you will have a solid guide to properly select what belongs, and discard what does not fit.

Who would you like to see in the story?

Each main character needs to start with a motto for life – a central guiding principle (in essence, their *personal* premise). Here are nine types of people to launch you off your diving board and into the water (based on a personality system called the *Enneagram*)...

1. The perfectionist – *I am always right.*
2. The pleaser – *I make others happy.*
3. The performer – *My image is everything.*
4. The reclusive artist – *I trust no one.*
5. The reclusive inventor – *I trust no one else's ideas.*
6. The appeaser – *I do what I am told.*
7. The fun-lover – *I do what I want to do.*
8. The bully – *I am the boss.*
9. The accommodator – *I bend to fit in.*

Within reason, we should see each main character to the extent that we know how they dress, where they prefer to live, and what rubs them the wrong way. These people didn't just pop out of thin air, and our characters must have a history – most of which only the writer knows about. Sketch a background story – something we call a 'backstory' – describing the most important events of each main character's life. Most of these details will never make it into our writing, and they are there to help us design our characters. In theory, our characters were alive before we met them, and our backstories can help us see them with greater clarity. Construct your characters in ways that intrigue you. Think of how they are unique, interesting, and larger than life. Give them the details of a life that is worthy of exploration.

It takes practice to create larger-than-life characters. It gets easier once you begin to see how the world is full of colorful building blocks. Most of us have clear memories of our parents, grandparents, or maybe a nutty uncle. We've had the chance to see our friends interacting with their own families. We've experienced plenty of co-workers, and we all know crazy, quirky, manic, annoying, weird, stupid, and brilliant people in real life – *these* people are the building blocks for our characters. Go to the mall. Go to a gospel church. Go to where people hang out. Listen and watch. Meanwhile, **ignore fictional characters** – these are not real people, and you'll only wind up making a *monstrously* imperfect copy of what somebody else has already imagined. Instead, build unique characters from the intriguing pieces of the interesting people you meet in life. They are out there. Believe me.

Based on memories floating around my head, I am constantly building fictional characters, and I seem to invent them long before I write about them. In fact, when enough of these characters show up in my mind, they begin to clamor for a story of their own …or at least it can feel that way. Often, my writing seems a lot like building a world for people who are looking for a home. But it isn't always that easy, and sometimes when I'm looking for someone fundamentally unusual, I'll produce a character using the following method…

When I see a human trait or mannerism or catchy way of speaking that grabs my attention, I'll make a mental note and jot this down as soon as I can. After collecting several dozen character traits – what I call 'blurbs,' I'll write these on individual Post-it notes and plaster my latest collection on a wall. Next, I'll grab handfuls of blurbs at random, and begin to read each one out loud, one-after-the-other without pausing. Finally, after I've read 5 or 10 or 15, I'll immediately ad lib a character sketch based on what I've just read, plus whatever else pops into my mind.

I imagine attributes like gender, age, what they do for a living, where they hang out, etc. And while I'm blabbing away, I'll drop blurbs that don't seem to fit and grab more to fill the missing pieces. It sounds nutty at first – but pressing ahead, I take each character sketch wherever it seems to be heading.

Often, this feels like a joke that is going nowhere fast …and in reality, this is often the case. At this point, nothing is cast in concrete, and it's fine to head in all sorts of directions. Eventually, I'll produce an amazing, unique, larger-than-life, yet entirely believable character – all derived from the real world.

With proper precautions, no one will be listening – except you. Let your imagination run wild. Now is the time to get creative!

Where would you like the story to happen?

Once the premise is set, and I have my main char–acters sketched out, the next most important decision is the physical setting. Although I've pieced some characters together, until I have a sense of where the story is taking place, I cannot effectively pin these people down. A military setting might infer a tendency toward a more regimented worldview, whereas a university setting might steer the characters toward a veneer of intellectual reserve and open-mindedness. As it turns out, people are largely defined by where they live, and until their world is properly defined, my characters rarely reveal a lot about themselves.

The personal opinions of my growing collection of characters and the overarching premise of the story can also suggest ideas for a setting. If the story is leaning toward a morality play and my characters are drawn to dilemmas and hard choices, then perhaps a religious setting might be effective. If my premise centers on notions of good versus evil, perhaps an authoritarian society might work.

Keeping the idea of a 'crucible' in mind (as discussed in Chapter 1), as a starting point I visualize real and specific places from my own personal experience. I don't just say 'the American Midwest.' Instead, I try pinning the setting down to a narrow locality such as 'the Orthodox Jewish section of Omaha, Nebraska.' I can always tweak the details later to disguise my setting. Or I can describe a genuinely real location.

There are advantages and disadvantages to setting my story in a real place. A real-world setting saves the trouble of inventing a fictitious world. On the other hand, trying to maintain 100% accuracy is like the guy who fills potholes for a living – there is always something not quite right. Ultimately, keeping everything straight is an endlessly distracting chore, and for this reason, I often borrow from the real world and sprinkle my fictitious settings with well-known elements. Settings of this sort produce a useful sense of authenticity without the prob– lem of getting everything right.

When writing fiction, filming a movie, or designing a video game, it is best to see the real world as a warehouse of elements ready to be imported – but *not* imported wholesale exactly the way we find them. Unless we have a reason to replicate an exact setting from history, it is best to mix and match fragments from the real world. Often, the most useful and realistic settings are combinations of two or three genuine locations. The familiarity of these places produces a sense of authen– ticity, but there is no need to depict details correctly. On the other hand, some locations are so well-known, there is no point in building a fictionalized version. The White House, the Mississippi River – places like these are typically imported intact.

If at all possible, once I begin to imagine my setting, I will physically go there, or at least to a similar place. With no particular method, I'll sniff the air and listen to the sounds – all to collect ideas while letting the place soak in. Returning to my writing software, I'll write about my version of this place in exquisite detail, ignoring what does not fit, and adding details that may not be true in the real world.

A single locality, or collection of localities, will grow to become the fictional world of my story. My audience will learn about this world through the eyes of my characters, and the way my characters interact with it. But at the very beginning of my writing, I do not build more than I need. Building a world takes time, and I begin with a basic outline for every setting. As the story grows, I insert details about the setting, but only to push the story along. Details that support the events of the story are added. Distracting details placed like window dressing must be avoided.

Just like the design of my characters, I *never* copy a setting from some other fictional story. If I do this, I'll wind up creating a second-rate setting based on my limited interpretation of somebody else's imagination. Instead, just like how I create characters from the real world, I collect snapshots from genuine places and design a setting based on real places. If I am designing a truly odd setting ...like living inside an asteroid – I will study what science tells us about asteroids.

Eventually, my setting begins to take on a life of its own, and my characters become accustomed to it. In fact, my characters will sometimes chime in on specific design details, and if my fictional world feels right to them, I'll keep adding details along those lines, and if they make a solid case that I am heading in the wrong direction, I'll rework the place. A character may also sometimes whine in a way that tells me that *he belongs there* – and in response, I tell him that this is *my world to create*, and I am the final arbiter of its suitability and authenticity. Eventually, my characters accept the fact of who I am – a sort of 'god' of their existence. They have a mission to perform, and the world I make for them is where this mission will take place. With respect to where they inhabit my story, I promise to treat them honestly and fairly – and nothing more.

The initial outlines of my setting are based on an eclectic collection of interesting details …a town clock that strikes its hours three minutes late …a bakery where someone keeps forgetting about pies smoldering inside their commercial oven …a flag flapping in the wind loud enough to hear. I'll sometimes draw a map, make pencil sketches of rooms and streets, and collect photographs of real places. I've even run a series of climate models to work out the consequences of a major calamity. Some of this will show up in my story, but not all of it. What matters most is how I have a place that's real to me, and a place where my characters can play out their lives.

When would you like this story to take place?

Another design parameter is the decision about *when* the story happens – in the past, the future, or contem–poraneously (or a mixture of all three). 'When' also includes the time before the story …the backstory and the total time period covered. The story may happen in just one afternoon, or across many generations. Time can be played out in any sequence. But no matter how we advance the story through time, the audience needs to clearly understand where they are on the timeline. For example, in a post-apocalyptic story, most of the action takes place after a collapse. It may also include flashbacks to a time prior to the currently messed up circumstances.

But temporal shifts can confuse the audience, and extra care must be taken to announce sudden shifts in time.

Sometimes the nature of a story confines the time to an obvious choice. For example, a sci-fi story may suggest a futuristic setting. On the other hand, some stories are timeless, and the setting can be mostly a matter of artistic preference. A story about human passion, conflicts over money, childrearing, a romantic comedy, or some other interpersonal topic can happen in a near-present age and there is little need to resurrect the past or construct a wholly fictional future. On the other hand, if I am focusing on horrendous consequences for mankind based on the poor decision-making of those in power, it might be better to select a truly dark moment from history or design a terrible future.

The advantages of a near-present-day time period include less effort replicating the deep past or imagining a realistic future. On the other hand, the near-present-day offers few unique settings that haven't been thoroughly explored, and keeping near-present-day details straight can become a constant distraction in the face of a well-informed audience.

Personally, I tend to set my 'present-day' stories 20 years in the future. In part, this allows me to avoid current events without the need to produce a wholly futuristic world. I also figure that 20 years from now – in the real future – few people will care about what I got wrong.

Ultimately, when to set our story depends on our expertise and interests. A historian may have no problem recreating an ancient setting, whereas a journalist might be more comfortable sticking with the present-day – and someone with a technological/scientific bent might feel entirely comfortable inventing a futuristic setting.

No matter what, the audience will be full of experts in history, current events, and technological trends, so we can't make this up willy-nilly. At the very least, no matter the time period, it's wise to research our setting enough to avoid glaring errors.

But forget about getting everything 100% dead nuts straight. No matter how hard we work, like rats nibbling on a live wire, purists will pick at every possible discrepancy. Sometimes, just to piss them off, I'll leave a minor inconsistency in a story. In fact, the movie, *Apollo 13* has a perfect example. Even though the art director clearly knew what the real Apollo 13 Saturn V rocket looked like, the movie version of the rocket has an obviously incorrect paint pattern. Partly, they may have done this to claim ownership of any future video clips floating around the internet, and I also suspect this was done as a way to thumb their nose at picky amateur space historians.

Our *real* audience includes people who show up to enjoy our stories, and as long as we design the details of time and place in a plausible way without glaring errors – *that is good enough.*

How do I pull these pieces into a story?

Once I have my premise worked out, my main characters outlined, and a tentative location and time–frame, I sketch out a rough concluding scene that 'proves the premise.' This scene will be rewritten many times, and the foundations of this scene will be added throughout the story. Yet once I have a tentative final scene in mind – the wording of my premise taped to my computer screen will begin to feel more like a real situation. The premise is no longer just words. From now on, I will imagine a final conflict that proves these words correct.

In *Return of the Jedi,* Luke defeats the dark side of the force. To do this, the story could have killed Darth Vader in battle – but the premise of *Star Wars* is not simply 'good *defeats* evil.' The premise has a subtle twist: 'Good *overcomes* evil.' In the end, Luke proves this premise by turning Vader away from his evil past, and the newly liberated Vader tosses the gobsmacked emperor to his doom – thereby proving the subtler meaning of the premise.

Keeping the temperature curve in mind (Chapter 3), once the protagonist begins to take on his nemesis, except during the climactic events at the end of the story, our hero will repeatedly fail. To produce my climactic scene, I write 8 to 10 *brief* sketches – a few paragraphs where the protagonist takes on the antagonist (a.k.a., 'skir–mishes'), and a brief reason for why the protagonist fails each time. I don't worry if these skirmishes are nearly the same or vastly different in temperature. I simply want to get the ball rolling.

Digging through these sketches, I set aside all but the best three to five, and rate them from least to most intense. Next, I place the second strongest sequence at the midpoint of the story. This will be rewritten to support the midpoint crisis. Finally, I lay out the rest of my skirmishes in ascending order of temperature all the way to the end of the story – placing the strongest last. After each skirmish (except the last), I include additional details describing how the protagonist gets tripped up or outmaneuvered by the antagonist. Only during the very last engagement will the protagonist finally win in a way that proves the premise.

Of course, I've just made a *huge* mess. None of my skirmishes connect. And so, right away, I'll rework each conflict – changing details until the events more-or-less string together into a workable sequence. Sometimes I'll rewrite an entire skirmish from scratch with entirely new material – or I'll split a sketch into two skirmishes or combine two into one.

Keep in mind that I am *still* writing sketches. Long ago, I learned to avoid lots of dialogue, setting description, or other secondary details until the basic sequence of the story is nailed down. Most of what I am writing will be tossed out later, and there is no point in writing a lot of detail that never makes it into the final draft.

Next, I sketch early scenes leading up to the midpoint crisis – quickly placing the protagonist and supporting characters into a bind that is clearly consistent with the basic conflict of the story and requires further investigation. In Episode 28, McCoy runs into the time portal and suddenly time is screwed up. But then what? We see the basic problem, but no clear solution.

At the end of *The Empire Strikes Back*, Luke pain–fully realizes that defeating Vader will not be as easy as a lightsaber fight. All the same, engaging Vader is the key. The early part of the story drives the protagonist toward the midpoint crisis – thereby forcing a painful choice the protagonist can no longer avoid. At the conclusion of the midpoint crisis, the protagonist realistically, genuinely, and fully commits to the central quest of the story (Chapter 3, Section 3.4).

From the end of the prologue all the way through the midpoint crisis, my protagonist and supporting characters face circumstances that are growing into an insurmoun–table dilemma …a deteriorating predicament with no resolution in sight. Meanwhile, the *antagonist* is also having many of the same sorts of problems. The prota–gonist and his team struggle to formulate a plan because the size of the problem keeps growing. Meanwhile, the antagonist is struggling with his own plans. In *Return of the Jedi*, Luke and his friends are worried about the empire closing on their position, while Vader is annoyed by a death star in no position to assert its reputation.

Even after the mid-point crisis, exactly how the protagonist will achieve the ultimate goal is still unclear. During the Council of Elrond in *The Lord of the Rings,* the reality of the situation grows as each council member speaks. In addition to the menace facing them, Frodo can see that everyone around him possesses a serious character defect – making each a potentially flawed ring-bearer. Meanwhile, Frodo has worn the ring around his neck for many days, and he hasn't yet succumbed to its power. Frodo had hoped to simply leave the ring with the elves and return home to the Shire. Now, he understands that he alone must bear the ring all the way to Mordor, and destroy it. No one else can do this, and if Frodo chooses to walk away, all of Middle Earth will fall into the hands of a dark and horrifying enemy. It is a monumental dilemma that can only be resolved if Frodo commits to the quest. As inconceivable as it seems to everyone present, the smallest among them will attempt the arduous task. Frodo will return the Ring of Power to Mount Doom, the only place in Middle Earth where the ring can be unmade.

This is the sort of midpoint we need in our story …like climbing a ladder to a diving board, standing on the board, and jumping. The first half of the story brings us to this point. The second half turns the commitment into action and a final resolution.

As already discussed, committing to the quest cannot be an easy choice – nor certain in its outcome. Opportunities to succeed will be slim. Potential failure will remain an unavoidable constant. There will be a price to pay for failure *or* success. And whether the protagonist wins or loses, the hero will be damaged by the quest and changed in ways that will never fully fade.

The commitment at the midpoint crisis ties the first half of the story (revealing the dilemma) into the second half of the story (working to accomplish the quest). With these two halves worked out, I'm almost done with my roughest of drafts. Finally, I will produce the very earliest scenes: the prologue, main character introductions, and the initial revelation of my premise (see Chapter 2). I won't bother with an epilogue until I complete a nearly final draft, and if possible, I will avoid an epilogue altogether.

Of course, even after producing a rough draft of my entire story, I still have a giant mess on my hands. Yet from this point forward I'll work out the details without worrying too much about the overall organization. The pieces are lined up and I am free to revise and add new content

If I were writing a novel, my rough draft at this point might be perhaps 60 to 80 pages and written to a level of detail much like a movie screenplay. If I were writing a screenplay or a script for a video game – I might have 20 to 30 pages sketched out.

The story now exists in a very rough form and it will take effort and dedication to turn this into a finished product. Yet the route has been established, a bulldozer has cleared the land for my road, the architectural plans are drawn, and the detailed construction is about to begin.

Next Up: Selecting the Details

Chapter 5
Selecting the Details

Making the simple complicated is commonplace. Making the complicated simple, awesomely simple, that's creativity.

— Charles Mingus

5.1. Saying more with less.

5.2. Motif.

5.3. References and Genre.

5.4. Comedy and tragedy.

5.5. Foreshadowing.

5.6. Character eccentricities.

5.7. Cloning characters.

5.8. Symbols.

5.1. SAYING MORE WITH LESS

Real life is far more complex than any story ever written. Even during the most mundane events, if I were to fully record what happens in its entirety, there wouldn't be enough room in any library to hold every last detail – and nobody would want to experience this mountain of information. For this reason, a story must be selective, concise, and brief.

A full-length motion picture screenplay contains about as much material as a 70-page novella, and runs on-screen for about two hours. A 300-page novel can be read comfortably over the course of a day, and a computer game can be completed in less than a week. By comparison, we live our lives on Earth for decades and engage dozens of new people each year.

How can I possibly create a rich story in just 70 pages? or 300 pages? or with 10 gigabytes of graphics, sound, and motion files?

We start by selecting the essential details, and we ignore everything else.

Instead of showing a 24/7/365 real life situation, we trim events to just a handful of representative scenes. Instead of portraying every minor or slightly major character who might possibly occupy a setting, we create a handful of memorable personalities who represent key aspects of the crowd.

Unavoidably, I always wind up spending 10% of my time hacking my rough draft into shape, and 90% tearing it to shreds and putting it back together again. Keeping simplicity in mind, I'll rework every detail – sometimes adding new material ...sometimes chucking entire scenes out the window. We want to tell our story with the most engaging and relevant details, and the remainder of this chapter describes the most common ways to say more with less.

5.2. MOTIF

Stories require lots of data. In fact, stories require perhaps *10,000 times* more data than any sensible nar–rative. How can we possibly include this much material without writing a story that fills a million pages?

In general, we attack this problem by reusing elements – themes, characters, settings, symbols, colors, catchphrases, etc. that are clearly introduced and appear again without introduction.

This sort of shorthand is called a **motif** [mow-TEEF]. For example, movie music themes are applied as a recurring motif – such as the brassy riff that plays just before Darth Vader shows up on-screen to spout his latest dastardly plan. With just a few notes, we almost don't even need to see this black-caped windbag. The music alone tells us that things are turning for the worse.

Early in Episode 28 of the original Star Trek series, we see Spock cover his Vulcan ears to avoid suspicion from 1930s New Yorkers *(as though they would ever notice!),* and while the story unfolds, Spock wears his hat to remind us about how far from home he and Kirk have traveled. Nothing more is said about the hat. It's just there on screen over-and-over reminding us about the odd circumstances of their quest. We also see Sulu injured by a flash of electrical sparks, and we see those same sparks again when Spock's memory circuit fails. Spock and Kirk steal clothes out of desperation, and later 'borrow' tools for the same reason. McCoy is always chewing his thumbnail when he is nervous. With a brief 'knowing' glance, Spock shows how he is constantly worried about Kirk's relationship with Edith, and how it might affect their mission.

Through motifs, more is said with less because the writer can insert previously introduced elements with no for further explanation. Meanwhile, the audience is tracking fewer unique details – keeping complexity at bay. And with recurring elements, this leads to fewer distractions and a story that feels increasingly familiar.

Unfortunately, the use of recurring motifs alone is not enough to limit the size of our story. What else can we do?

5.3. REFERENCES and GENRE

The constant goal of saying more with less is as simple as it is demanding: We need to reduce the comp–lexity and size of our story while keeping the story intact. Producing our own recurring elements requires an introduction, and there isn't enough room to introduce every element in our story. Motifs can help, but introducing more than a handful of motifs uses more space than we can afford.

We clearly need something to insert right out of the box, something like a *pre-made* motif that needs no introduction. In fact, we do this all the time when we refer to motifs in famous stories, or widely-experienced elements from the real world. For example, if I were to insert the first few notes from the *Star Spangled Banner* and noise from a ballpark, I might invoke the complex atmosphere of a baseball game with all of its associated elements.

Rather than a lengthy sequence showing a character reacting to a new circumstance, the character might simply invoke a quick reference like "I don't think we're in Kansas anymore..." in this case, a line lifted straight from *The Wizard of Oz*. By inserting a well-known line from a famous story, we can infuse huge amounts of data without introducing anything from scratch.

This helps quite a bit. But even pre-made references consume time and space. To further reduce the comp–lexity of our story, we often let the audience do some of the work. Rather than inserting *anything* – when the exact details don't matter, we leave space for the audience to imagine the details for themselves.

For example, assuming our characters can find their way around, routine travel sequences are rarely included. Even wild sci-fi explanations are often ignored – like how a futuristic space ship travels among the stars. We don't need this explained because *Star Trek* and *Star Wars* and a host of other sci-fi space stories have already produced ready-to-use standard-issue solutions for faster-than-light space travel. Why invent a new method? Why even bring this up? Give it the gas, hit the magic red button, and head out into space.

Like the expectation of 'hyperspace' travel in a fut–uristic sci-fi adventure, well-known motifs are widely associated with similar stories – collectively known as a *genre* [ZHON-ra]. Specifically, a storytelling genre focuses on one of several dozen well-known settings, topics, or themes. Examples include… fantasy, science fiction, horror, western, romance, thriller, mystery, detec–tive, and dystopia – each with its own set of ready-to-use expectations. A saloon comes with saloon etiquette. A haunted house looks like a haunted house. And by writing in a particular genre, we can build our story inside a ready-made soup of recognizable elements.

When we write within a specific genre, our story takes on an immediate level of familiarity, and where these elements can appear without any introduction or background explanation, this frees up space to develop unique elements that pertain solely to the details of our specific story. Talk about saying more with less!

5.4. COMEDY and TRAGEDY

Gazing all the way back to the beginning of story–telling, every story falls into two basic genres …comedy and tragedy. In fact, the whole happy-face/sad-face motif associated with live theater originates with the ancient Greeks who made a big point about this distinction. Before we write a single word, we need to make a choice

– is our story a *comedy* or a *tragedy?* Our choice must be unambiguous, and it can't change once the story begins.

Although stories may briefly reach across the comedic/tragic divide to ease tension or reduce a sense of fluff – once the die has been cast, no story should *ever* completely transition the comedic/tragic boundary. There is simply no way for an audience to process this transition. If they find themselves laughing at a genuine tragedy, or crying over a joke – you'll royally piss them off and they will never trust you again. The movie *Galaxy Quest* falls into this trap. It begins as a farce before veering into a quasi-serious story. By the time the crew is in mortal danger, the audience does not know whether to fear for their lives or laugh at the implausibility of their situation.

Comedic elements are sometimes used to lighten a tragedy, and tragic elements are sometimes used to keep a comedy attached to the real world. For example, in the *Star Wars* movies, all kinds of hilarious lines are yelled during the heat of battle – especially when Han Solo is around. Yet the *Star Wars* series is clearly a tragedy – made entirely obvious when Luke's family is murdered by stormtroopers early in the first movie. The ground–breaking TV series *MASH,* on the other hand, is a comedy that often includes serious material (and sometimes entire episodes without a laugh track) in order to keep the story focused on realistic characters in a tough situation. *Men in Black* drifts closer to the line, yet it's clearly a comedy, albeit on the dark side considering how it includes several brutal murders.

A comedy is a comedy, and a tragedy is a tragedy. Pick one, then borrow elements from the other to keep your story emotionally balanced (not too dark, not too much fluff).

5.5. FORESHADOWING

A well-written story includes more than a sequence of events. It is a fully stocked *storehouse of essential information* that offers a host of critical storytelling clues including character traits, recurring motifs, setting attributes, familiar scenes from other stories, genre assumptions, references to the real world, and even assumptions about the general knowledge of our audience. Early in our story, all the way to the midpoint crisis, we plainly reveal this information for later use.

Once we pass the midpoint crisis, there will be no time or space to reveal anything that hasn't been revealed already. The storehouse of information teaches the audience about our premise, our characters, the quest, and the antagonist's opposition – and pre-plants information ready for action at a moment's notice. Most importantly, we reveal material that will prepare the audience to experience the conclusion of the story as deeply and directly as possible.

This educational process is called *'foreshadowing.'*

Like lumber delivered ahead of carpenters who arrive later to build a house, foreshadowing is a process where we deliberately preplace story elements before they are utilized in later scenes. Preplaced elements offer a glimpse of what *might* happen and they remove the need for explanations later when too much is happening to reveal anything new. In *Men in Black*, the 'red button' is revealed very early, and it will clearly play an essential role at some point in the story. The audience has no idea when this will happen, but they will be ready when the button comes into play.

Properly foreshadowed stories preplace every single element, often repeating these elements in multiple ways. As the story progresses, scenes should be like a 10-piece jigsaw puzzle where we've already been staring at the first nine pieces …and finally, the last and only possible piece falls into place. A ship that sinks right after it first appears is like a bubble that bursts right after it forms. Who cares about that ship? On the other hand, if the audience has been fully exposed to the crew's disregard for the weather, the sinking is plausible, sensible, and logically satisfying.

This is not to say the audience understands the nature of the missing piece. But they can see the empty spot, and they know that sooner or later something will fill this space. Sometimes the final piece is obvious. Sometimes it's something fitting, yet unexpected. Being caught off guard can be an awesome moment for an audience, and a sudden plot twist is fine as long as it is preplaced on *some* level. A major car crash, for example, might be a critically pivotal turning point that shocks the audience. Yet without the slightest pre-planted clue placed ahead of time – such as a kid crashing his toy car during the prologue – there is no way for the audience to absorb the event when it happens. No matter how much we want to shock our audience, we need to install the final piece of the puzzle from their stockpile of preplaced clues.

Nothing interesting or meaningful ever happens out of the blue, and there should always be multiple preplaced elements underlying every scene in our story. Otherwise, our audience cannot absorb the meaning of what they are seeing. Without foreshadowing, the audience will break their immersion bubble, withdraw to their thoughts, and work out the significance of what is happening based on pure speculation. In other words – we just lost our audience.

As a storyteller, *'plant it early and plant it often'* are words to live by. In every way possible, when something happens in our story, it needs to happen based on elements that are previously revealed. For example, in the first scene in the movie, *Jason Bourne*, we see a little kid shadow boxing. Throughout the entire movie, there will be a lot of punching, including the climactic scene. The tiny vignette of the kid is seemingly insignificant, but this plants an essential visual image right from the beginning of the movie. The meaning has yet to emerge, but the audience is already expecting at least one fist-fight later in the story.

Ultimately, we cannot tell a satisfying story by with–holding information. Imagine a grubby hand prying open a door when the audience knows that a nearby prison escape is underway. The hand would add a terrifying detail. Leave the prison escape element out, and the audience might imagine just about anything ...including a car mechanic who accidentally locks himself out of his house. Without clearly planted clues, the audience has no idea how to interpret the flow of events.

Remember what I write about the prologue (Chapter 2). *The audience has no idea what anything means until it plays out inside our story.* Piling on motifs and pre-planted possibilities does not spill the beans. *Not one bit.* Instead, foreshadowing adds pieces to the puzzle, thereby educating our audience to understand what they are exp–eriencing in the moment. When a final piece falls into place, it arrives in full view of every supporting element, and this communicates enormous meaning.

Like the motto of many indigenous New World nations, '*nothing goes to waste,*' I will often reuse the elements of an earlier scene in a future scene. For example, in Episode 28 of the original Star Trek series, we see many foreshadowed events... Spock berates himself for failing to record history while it flashes through the time machine annulus. Kirk dives for McCoy just when McCoy runs into the portal, hitting the deck hard with his arms wrapped around thin air. Kirk and Spock escape from a New York City cop with Kirk saying, "let's get out of here!" Of course, early in the story, the conclusions of these three scenes are fairly straightforward. Later, they add enormous depth. Spock's tricorder is central to their success, Kirk grabs for McCoy with a bear-hug that keeps McCoy from saving Edith, and just after traveling back to their own time, Kirk once again talks about leaving – but this time adds the 'h' word for emphasis (which almost kept this episode from airing in 1967).

The other day, I saw a great example of fore–shadowing on a poster for the original 1968 movie *Planet of the Apes*. Painted in exquisite detail, we see the final climactic semi-mind-blowing scene of the entire movie. Yet without knowing the story, nothing is spoiled, and instead, the image is solidly planted for maximum impact.

Review everything that will happen throughout your entire story and work to ensure that elements are pre-placed and ready to support everything that follows. Through foreshadowing, the audience will recognize key events for what they are, and remain fully immersed and engaged.

5.6. CHARACTER ECCENTRICITIES

In terms of revealing information, our characters are the most complicated elements of our story. Characters typically only do or say what is appropriate in the mom–ent, and a storyteller can't merely operate them like a puppet.

I often tackle this problem starting with two basic elements… mannerisms and catchphrases. With a simple gesture or recurring tagline, I can let a character's state of mind leak into the story without a lot of complicated dialog. For example, Han Solo has a 'bad feeling' about a lot of things, C3P0 shuffles along and gets flustered throughout every Star Wars movie, and notice how much mileage the filmmakers achieve using R2D2's various whistles and techno-squeaks.

Other than working to ensure that characters align to their personal premises, there are no limits on manner–isms and catchphrases. Ultimately, we let our characters become who they are, and reveal themselves as much as they are willing. Meanwhile, we keep an eye open for personal eccentricities that can offer a shortcut. Character behavior is complex. Everyone is different, and all of this leaks out eventually.

To compress the flow of our story, every character exhibits useful mannerisms and catchphrases. Even subtle characters like Mr. Spock will say 'fascinating,' and lift an eyebrow now and again. We just need to let our characters reveal their eccentricities to us.

5.7. CLONING CHARACTERS

Sometimes storytellers will harmonize a collection of characters by inventing two or three main personality archetypes – then clone each of these archetypes into several characters at different ages (or even different gen–ders). The boy, the man, the grandfather, and the cousin can sometimes arrive in our story as the same basic character seen at different stages in their lives. In essence, we are applying the theory of 'motif' to the design of our characters.

Over time, cloned characters can take different paths, and evolve unique aspects. Yet by starting with the same basic personality archetype, the common elements of each character clone-set can bring about a quick sense of familiarity, thereby saving time and space we would otherwise dedicate to developing individual characters.

Nothing beats a great character more than having the same character in many forms. Is not Obi-Wan Kenobi merely an older and wiser version of Luke Skywalker? (Or George Lucas, for that matter). Can we really see a difference between the emperor and Darth Vader in most scenes? The 'wizard' in the Wizard of Oz shows up in all sorts of manifestations. In many stories, the 'son' and 'father,' the 'master' and 'apprentice,' the 'teacher' and 'student,' the 'therapist' and 'client' are all very much the same people at different stages of their development.

Since we are telling a story and not a true family history, we have the freedom to clone our characters into an instant character motif system. And through this process, we can compress and enrich our stories much like how we apply any other motif system.

If your story needs to include a dozen fleshed-out characters, try creating several thoroughly interesting personalities, then slice them into clones, and introduce them at different stages of their lives. They will be different people, but your ensemble will remain manageably familiar.

5.8. SYMBOLS

Creating motifs and shortcuts can take many forms – sometimes purely symbolic. In *Men in Black*, we see bugs everywhere because the antagonist is a bug. In *Star Wars*, a lightsaber is strongly associated with a Jedi knight (or a dark-side Sith). In *ET*, the plant is dying …then it is suddenly revived, and right away we know the alien is alive. In *Apollo 13*, Jim Lovell watches his crewmates staring at the passing lunar surface from the window of their lunar module lifeboat, and without saying a word, we know what this means – Jim will never land on the Moon. Typically, our audience will respond to a symbol more directly and viscerally than to anything else they see. Symbols save time, yet more than this, symbols can illustrate a powerful idea without using words.

In *Apollo 13*, the story begins with the launch-pad fire of Apollo 1, famously killing all three astronauts. While the entire movie unfolds, we see forms of fire at every major turning point. It shows up again when Jim Lovell explains the risks to his family. It comes up during problems with their training. We see lots of fire during the launch of the massive Saturn V rocket. We see it again when their service module oxygen tank explodes, and once more when they burn their lunar module descent engine for a critical course correction – and finally, during the climactic sequence, like a human-occupied meteor, we see the fire of reentry when their command module plows into the Earth's atmosphere at 35,210 feet per second. By now, everyone involved is worried about a potentially defective heatshield – and a fiery death. More than the space environment, the inability of NASA to readily control and properly protect the astronauts from *fire* is the central antagonist of this movie. Even the problem of CO_2 poisoning is a 'combustion' problem of sorts, since metabolism is nothing more than a low-intensity fire.

In short, with respect to this entire chapter... Consider every element of your story to see how you might reuse every piece. Once you are weaving your entire story with familiar elements, you will have enough space to tell your story all the way to a satisfying conclusion.

Next Up: Re-Writing – What we Really Do!

Chapter 6

Re-writing – What We Really Do!

It is not enough to do your best; you must know what to do, and THEN do your best. – W. Edwards Deming

6.1. BURIED ORDNANCE

Once the basics are in place ...prologue, characters, premise, setting, foreshadowing, initial dilemma, mid–point crisis, the quest, skirmishes, and conclusion – the storyteller's task switches to fixing, reworking, and cleaning up the mess... We toss out the garbage, add new (and better) material, and polish every element. Everything we write can benefit from rewriting. Or said the way it comes to mind – we call our earliest writing a '*rough* draft' for a reason.

Ernest Hemingway famously claimed to rewrite portions of his books up to 50 times before releasing anything for public consumption. In this age of spell-checkers and other digital tools, I could almost hear that as a joke – except that it usually takes me dozens of major editing sessions to straighten out my own writing. In case you are wondering, while I am polishing the latest edition of this book, I've been rewriting 1/3 of my sentences, and some of these up to a dozen times.

Trying to improve any work of art can just as easily ruin it, and rewriting is always an unclear path. As a start, I save a backup copy of my file in several places. If you are not yet making copies of your work on multiple drives in multiple locations, *stop reading this book now* – and set this up. When it comes to safeguarding our work, we should not be trusting the 'cloud' ...Apple, Google, Amazon, or Facebook. Save your work on the cloud, but also save it locally. At the very least, buy a pair of external drives and several USB memory sticks, and back up your work every day. If you lose a file or decide you don't like yesterday's edits, you'll need a backup copy – and to ensure you never lose your work – *many* backups. Don't take any chances. Thousands of hours of work might be at stake.

I start the rewriting process by working through my story beginning to end. Once I've reviewed the entire story, I edit random chapters and randomly edit sections inside each chapter. The goal here is to see the story nonlinearly, and this leads to a process I describe in terms of 'weaving' – and nothing weaves a story together better than moving freely through the text in any direction. By bouncing around, I arrive with other parts of the story clearly in mind – offering a chance to plant clues and universal motifs, and it also tends to standardize my writing style. If editing turns into a slog, the writing will take on that feeling, and once I am growing tired of an editing method, I'll try something else to keep me on my toes. Scanning for the same word used throughout the text can offer a fresh look, and I'll even search for everyplace I've used a dash or a comma.

Eventually, I return to a front-to-back edit and have my computer read large sections of text at a time. MS Word on Windows 10 reads out loud almost as well as I do, and this is a fantastic way to listen for typos, missing words, and awkward language. I assume that other systems are equally able to convert text to speech – and it is certainly worth a try, even if you are a skilled proofreader.

In addition to clumsy word-use, I am looking for incomplete thoughts, illogical connections, and structural issues. Where the computer reads what it sees, problems are easy to notice. Once I can read my story end-to-end without stopping every two seconds to fix a problem – I am done with my first draft. Why not *entirely* done? Because this is my own viewpoint. The biggest rewriting hurdles stem from our own blind spots – problems we do not see, and therefore cannot fix. When other people read my work, they will find all sorts of problems I didn't notice.

A video game script is a working document that changes throughout production, and it doesn't require meticulous professional editing, but this is no excuse to leave my work unpolished. To reveal hidden problems, I send early drafts to trusted readers who offer critical feedback. In the 'biz,' these people are called 'beta-readers.' Finally, I'll toss the text into free software like *Grammarly* that searches for innocuous typos. Software cannot write your story, and I do not agree with most of what it finds, but it can find a lot of bugs no one else is seeing.

Normally, I don't define anything by 'what it is not.' Yet the rewriting process is much more about rooting out common mistakes than adding better material. In this chapter, I mostly address mistakes that have shown up in my own writing. Your own mileage may differ.

6.2. REAL-TIME EDITING

While writing brand new material, my creative pro–cess is mostly unaware of my writing mistakes. In fact, while typing right now, I am taking my best shot at saying what I want to say. But until I switch into editing-mode, I am unable to see how well this is going.

Real-time editing involves rapidly switching bet–ween new material and making edits along the way. In my own work, I typically switch modes at the end of each new sentence. I need to edit while producing new mat–erial. Otherwise, looking back on this later, I may not understand what I was trying to say. If I am not editing often enough, I may write an entire section that winds up trashed because I didn't notice how I'd already developed this material earlier, or made some other major mistake. On the other hand, if I drop into editing mode *too* often, I can lose my train of thought and miss a chance to work out a unique idea.

While flipping between writing and editing modes, I'm mainly looking for glaring problems related to my story. Does the sentence make sense in terms of the setting? Are my characters behaving according to their personal premises? Does the action line up with recent events? Has all of this material been sufficiently foreshadowed?

Once an entire paragraph or sequence of dialog is finished, I'll step back and read it. Looking for missing words, repetition, and other annoying problems, I may re–phrase a sentence or two. I am not editing. I am repairing the most glaring problems. As long as my thoughts are reasonably intact – and clear enough to understand later – this is enough for now.

My early drafts will require detailed and extensive revisions that may continue for days, weeks, months, or years. But that is no surprise. Re-writing our stories over-and-over is where we spend most of our time as story–tellers. And if we care about our writing, there is no way around this reality.

6.3. EDITING IN DETAIL

Before I say anything more about editing – by far, the most important point to keep in mind on the topic of editing is as simple as it gets: *You are the final editor*. Professional editors can flag problems and offer useful feedback …helping us to focus on what needs attention. But they will never see the story as clearly as the storyteller. And we should never ask an editor to turn a rough-draft into finished text. Once editors begin to re-write sections of our story – they are no longer 'editors' – they are co-authors. This may be what you want, but if you let this happen, you are no longer in control of your story. Feedback is essential, and as the sole storyteller, I'll accept input from anyone who helps me polish my work, but I will never relinquish my authorship. In fact, this is the main reason why I stopped writing screenplays. Typically, a screenwriter has no final say in how the story is produced. To a lesser extent, this is true in all published writing and video game production. But if your story is solid and well-edited, you have a much better chance of seeing your work published the way you wrote it.

Before I attempt any major editing, I'll often let a story sit for a few days, weeks, months, or even years. Reading a printed-paper version or having my computer read the text out loud can help. Sometimes, I'll publish a draft on a private website and read it online using a web browser with what feels like a fresh set of eyes.

If you feel that this editing process is never-ending – you are not alone. *Non-fiction* is bounded by the reality of the genuine world, whereas *fiction* is bounded by our limitless imagination. In fiction-writing, there is no nat–ural end to the editing process because nothing about our imaginary story precludes any sort of change on any sort of scale. In a nutshell – editing a fictional story only ends when we decide we are done.

6.4. COMMON WRITING PROBLEMS

The editing minefield is littered with all sorts of potential disasters. Ham-handed editing that worries too much about things like classical fifth-grade grammar and word-precision is one of the more popular ways to mangle the flow and artistry of a story. But not the only way. Occasionally, I'll write something that makes perfect sense to me – yet little sense to anyone else, and only feedback from other people will make me aware of this. Sometimes my editing is too conservative. Sometimes too aggressive. One of my favorite tools involves a meat cleaver – 'when in doubt chop it out.' But this can get me into trouble because sometimes I'll chop out something that should have stayed put. I keep older versions of my writing. But once a major section vanishes, its connection to the story often melts away, and it is no easy task to restore it later.

Here are the most common mines in the editing minefield:

Dialogue Instead of Action

Dialogue is no substitute for a character's decisive‐ness, actions, or reactions. Dialogue can color their per‐sonalities and round out the edges of who they are, and dialogue can confirm and punctuate what the audience already understands. Yet as much as possible, dialog should never reveal anything important, and as much as possible, the audience should learn about what is hap‐pening from the non-verbal elements of our story. This does not imply that characters should never speak. It means that the storyteller must *reveal what is happening* before anything meaningful can be said about it. In short, to cite a common writer's rule …don't make the characters tell the audience what is happening. Instead, *show* the audience what is happening.

Dialogue always has far more impact when mixed with action. Han Solo's pithy remarks in the heat of battle clearly reveal his bravado-laced insecurities, whereas the same remarks would drop dead on the floor if nothing much were happening at the time. The famous line from *Gone with the Wind* is one of the best examples of dialogue reinforcing what we already know... "Frankly, my dear, I don't give a damn!" where Rhett offers a parting statement to Scarlett that is nothing more than a giant exclamation point pinned to a foregone conclusion.

The popular notion of 'stories in video games' imagines a host of dialogue-rich movie clips and other non-interactive 'cut-scene' material. Yet pausing the game to tell the story is the worst solution. Instead of pulling players into the game, dialogue-rich supplementary material pushes them out. The most effective storytelling in a video game places the entire story inside the world of the game, and there is never a reason to leave the game to absorb what is happening.

In my own experience, when designing my game mod, *A Keeper of the Prophecies,* I assembled a 'round table' of player experts to critique my proposal for the last major section of the campaign. My original design relied heavily on something we call a 'camvator' where I planned to attach the player's view to an invisible moving platform. Camvators would carry the player on a tour through the final few scenes of the story, and the player would watch the last 10 or 15 minutes of the game like a giant cut scene – no choices to make, nothing left to do.

My committee soundly rejected this proposal – instead insisting that the player should roleplay as long as possible. In the end, I produced two brief camvators and kept the player as an active agent for all but the last few minutes.

In video games, player-actions always speak louder than sitting around watching something from the sidelines, and if you include cut-scenes in your game, the videos should always contain actions more than words, and return the player to roleplaying mode as soon as reasonably possible.

In short – tell your story through events, immediate situations, conflicts, dilemmas, and time-limited sequences that do not offer a respite for the characters (or the game player). And only let your character speak in ways that confirm what the audience already strongly suspects.

Sacred Cows

Early in my writing career, I would begin a story by jotting down a powerful scene or sequence of scenes – and the rest of the story would be written around this core. Later, out of pure sentimentality, I would often refuse to substantially edit this core – almost like a sacred cow. A sacred cow can be any length, sometimes a sentence, a paragraph, or several pages. At first, a sacred cow can feel like a pot of glue holding the whole story together. Yet sacred cows rarely help to prove my premise, and by taking up space and sending the story into a dead-end street, they tend to drag the whole story down.

By 'a sacred cow' I am mainly referring to those trite and often unbelievable contrivances that we see in many bad stories …a totally implausible subplot or disconnected dialog that exists to hold the monster together while it writhes through the projection machine, or across the pages of a book, or through the course of some terrible computer game. 'Glue' is never part of a story. Glue is an encapsulating tumor that has no connection to the story at all.

Like Frankenstein's monster, my sacred cows become sutured to my story – even though there is no reason for their existence. And due to endless exposure, I can no longer imagine the story without them. The longer sacred cows stick around, the longer my story will remain adrift, and until these things are pitched overboard, every new effort is a waste of time.

This is not to say that writing random scenes is a bad idea early in the creative process. I write a lot of rough material in search of new ideas. But once I know what I want to say, I set everything aside that does not fit – no matter how much I like it.

In short – once you know what you want to say, drop *everything* that does not belong.

High-Concept

'High-concept' is not a classical story. Instead, it takes the form of a 'what if' statement like… "What if gravity suddenly disappeared?" or "What if there were a volcano in downtown Los Angeles?"

High-concept yarns typically toss incompatible characters into outrageously awkward circumstances and force them to confront the same ridiculous scenario over and over throughout the entire movie, book, or game. There are few famous examples because few garner any lasting notice. If forced to name examples, I'd say *Snakes on a Plane* and just about any slasher or zombie movie ever made.

High concept does not make a point, and it is nothing more than a fixed formulation that cannot be challenged in any fundamental way without shattering the "what if" tagline.

High-concept circumstances never attempt to prove anything. Instead, they are devices that explore a recur–ring gag or an absurd situation. This forces the characters to behave in unconventional and often painfully embarrassing ways. And this is supposedly entertaining.

High-concept tales attempt to tickle the audience with a disorienting and disquieting experience – like a rollercoaster ride with no safety belt. There is no point other than the uncomfortable nature of the ride itself. Just about every Adam Sandler film fits this description.

A volcano erupts in downtown LA. People run around screaming. Then a *bigger* eruption happens. More people run around screaming. Then a *bigger* eruption…

At the end of a high-concept story, an absolutely absurd contrivance is produced that 'fixes the problem' – solely because the abomination needs to end.

There are rare examples of successful stories that are somewhat high-concept in nature. *Men in Black,* for example, asks 'what if the tabloids are true?' However, this story works as a *story* because of how the concept is retooled as a premise: The tabloids are true. Space aliens live on the Earth. Our world is saved from alien forces on a regular basis. Rather than repeating the same gag over and over, the structure of *Men in Black* drives to a conclusion that clearly demonstrates the premise of the story.

A high-concept production never proves anything beyond showing how many ways the situation can produce a confusing mess in the lives of fictitious people. This may be what the audience wants – a good laugh or fright at the expense of tormented characters. Yet typically, this material would work much better within a classically-structured story.

If you want to write a satisfying story, make sure you are working toward proving your premise. And if you haven't yet defined your premise. Stop. You may be writing a high-concept ball of yarn that winds up going nowhere.

Melodrama

A melodrama is a situational exercise that masquerades as a story. Characters in a melodrama never rise above the level of 2D stereotypes. In order to fill the vast empty space normally occupied by 3D characters, they overplay everything about themselves. Placed in the role of main characters, stereotypical characters have no business drawing this much attention, but they are here anyway.

A soap opera is a typical example. Everything happens in endlessly overt detail, and everyone overreacts because almost nothing is happening. The episodes drag along to where little is left to the imagination. Every circumstance is pumped to the max for no sensible reason. The patient has cancer, a bad heart, liver trouble, looming bankruptcy, girlfriend problems, and a contract on his life – all at the same time. And *still*, we don't care one bit about this character.

The entire point is simply to push beyond all plausibility …forcing impossible *papier-mâché* charac‐ ters into impossible *papier-mâché* situations. There is no premise, and for this reason, there can be no clear resolution to any dilemma. The yarn is nothing more than a worn-out confabulation that simply *exists*.

Under very narrow circumstances, melodramatic methods can be made to work as a *brief* device. A deliberate farce, for example, is a melodramatic method used to illustrate a point through overt exaggeration (perhaps the TV series, *The Office*, and the *Airplane!* series of movies). But even a well-played farce is rarely as satisfying as a story that plays it straight. The best stories follow the lives of well-developed three-dimensional characters who are seeking a genuinely important goal while facing credible obstacles.

Anticlimax

The strongest scene in our story is located at the climactic end. Our story reaches an 'anticlimax' when the temperature of a mid-story scene peaks higher than its final climactic scene and 'steals the show.'

I once had a powerful scene midway through a screenplay where the protagonist escapes doom in an outstandingly dramatic fashion. Unfortunately, as I discovered, nothing after that point was going to top this moment. After trying everything I could imagine to beef up the end of the story – all to no avail – I toned down the earlier scene. If I hadn't done that, the end of the story would have felt like a lame afterthought, and the story would have ended in a whimper.

An anticlimax can also take place when too much material is stuffed into an epilogue. An epilogue with too many moving parts can seem like the story isn't quite over – like maybe a surprise ending is right around the corner. Instead of tying up loose ends, a bloated epilogue drains the life from our climactic ending. For example, the last book in the *Lord of the Rings* series has exactly this problem where several main characters return to the Shire after their great victory, and spend a host of days mopping up a nettlesome situation loosely extending from the central events. After so much devastation elsewhere in Middle Earth, maybe Tolkien felt that the Shire shouldn't escape a destructive fate. At any rate, it turns into a 50-page slog that I was happy never made it into the final movie.

In short, limit the size of your epilogue, and stick to the temperature curve by keeping the intensity of your climactic conclusion at the highest point of your entire story.

Explaining

If anything needs to be explained – do it very early. And if the explanation is taking too long, simplify it, or see if you can leave it out altogether. Audiences are smarter and more insightful than writers typically imagine, and sometimes we need to have faith in their ability to cite their own experience. Often, the audience won't care about the technicalities at all. For example, is it really necessary for George Lucas to tell us in *Star Wars: Episode 1* exactly how 'The Force' works? ...or show us a cute-looking kid who will one day turn into the big bad Darth Vader? Give it a rest.

Stories should never stop to tell the audience what is happening. Everything worth knowing at every point should be planted in plain view before anything important happens. For example, in James Cameron's movie *Titanic*, there is an early scene where we learn about the technicalities of how the ship sinks from a modern computerized perspective. Later, we see this happening during the actual sinking of the ship, and because we were exposed to the basic physics early in the story, there is no need to freeze-frame the film while somebody explains why the ship just broke in half. The story keeps rolling because we already know why this happens.

If you must explain a key concept – for the sake of your audience – only explain what really needs to be understood, and do this as *early* as possible so it doesn't slow down the action once events begin to heat up.

Incestuous Writing

I am always nauseous to hear songs sung about songs, paintings painted about paintings, or poetry written about poetry. And I'm more than a bit nervous when a video game character is a game player. 'Incestuous writing' happens when the storytelling experience is the topic of the storytelling experience. For me, it feels like the artist is sheltered and disconnected from reality, and has absolutely nothing to say.

Of course, by writing this book on the topic of writing, I tread close to my self-imposed taboo. But I won't write a *story* about the life of a person writing a story unless absolutely necessary – like stories that have been written about the struggles of Virginia Woolf, where she happens to be a writer, and there's no avoiding that connection.

If all of our ideas revolve around sitting at a keyboard – the time has come for us to see the world, and when we return from our real-life adventures, we can begin with fresh insight. Living in the real world is the only advice I can offer to cure a case of incestuous writing.

Not about People

Perhaps the easiest mistake happens when we forget that every story is bounded by human nature …that it must revolve around the lives of genuinely human characters. For this reason, stories must be *anthro–pomorphic*, which means that no matter who the characters are, they are *always* human in terms of their personalities. The characters may not look like humans. But without exception, they must have human charac-teristics – even if they are aliens.

Next Up: Can a Great Story be told in a Game?

Chapter 7

Can a Great Story Be Told in a Game?

The farther back you can look, the farther forward you are likely to see. – Winston Churchill

7.1. The quick answer.

7.2. The longer answer.

7.3. History.

7.4. The way ahead.

7.5. Suggestions.

7.6. Parting shot.

7.1. THE QUICK ANSWER

(Can a great story be told in a game?)

For the last 15-20 years the answer has been 'yes,' as long as game designers build a story into their game that follows the basic rules of classical storytelling.

7.2. THE LONGER ANSWER

A game can never be a story in and of itself, any more than a story can function as a game. They each produce unique and overlapping experiences. One is passive; the other interactive. One is where I root for the hero; the other is where *I am* the hero. Much like the division between comedy and tragedy, at its core, the thing is either a story or a game – one or the other. The builder / designer / writer decides which, and then how much to include of the other.

Telling a story in a game is possible because a story does not preclude gameplay and gaming does not pre–clude storytelling. More than anything else, story–telling in a game requires a working knowledge of human storytelling hardwiring, and a willingness to make these rules operate inside an interactive media setting.

Many games include hours of video, and it might be argued that a game with this much passive material does a 'good job' of storytelling – but external cut scenes are *movies* – not stories built into the game.

At the other extreme, we see massive multiplayer internet games like *Fortnite* and *League of Legends* that ignore the basic structure of a story altogether. Endless games like these use storytelling elements to produce an engaging player experience. But an endless game cannot drive toward a final conclusion that proves a premise – the central element of storytelling.

A game is primarily an interactive experience with a goal. That sounds a lot like storytelling. But working toward a goal is not necessarily a story. If we are going to call something a story, the ongoing events of the game must approximate a storytelling structure (a.k.a., chapters 1 through 6), and our protagonist (a.k.a., the player's gameplay avatar) must resolve a fundamental conflict that proves a clear and well-revealed premise. Proving a premise is a goal. But accomplishing a goal does not necessarily prove a premise.

7.3. HISTORY

There was a time when video games did not tell a story ...or at least not in the way that I've been talking about in this book. There are nonetheless story elements in 1980s games such as *Pac Man* and *Pong*. As players of those games, we identify an adversary – the ghosts, or the other Pong player, and we experience a continuous conflict where staying alive is the main point.

Simulating real-life produced virtual settings and characters, and in the early 1990s, we began to build imaginary places inside *Sim City* and *Sim Farm*, and we watched how these settings responded to our inputs. Later, *The Sims* opened the door to interactions with real people inside invented places. Yet none of this was more than hanging out at a pizza party. There was no protagonist or antagonist, no premise to prove, no effort to resolve anything. In fact, the whole point of *The Sims* was less focused than *Pac Man*. Survival was taken for granted, and for the most part, there was nothing to gain or lose.

Near the end of the 1990s, early first-person shooter games like *Quake* and *Doom* included automated adver–saries. A tiny bit of implausible backstory was also presented, and the player got to fight for goals, but the goals were mainly 'gaming goals' rather than story goals – like 'take this building' or 'capture this flag.' Working toward each goal, players faced automated conflicts, and this produced rising tension like a story – but fighting for a goal without character-driven motivations – this omitted the powerful punch of a story. At the conclusion of games like *Quake* and *Doom* – without the satisfaction of an emotional resolution and pay-off – the players had a sense of achievement, but no sense of meaningful significance.

At the turn of the 21st Century, incarnations of *Half Life*, *Halo*, and a host of other third-generation games produced a deeper backstory and a higher level of story complexity. Players found themselves in somewhat realistic settings, and they faced generally plausible dilemmas. The main characters were relatively normal in their abilities, and more than scoring points, their goals were about pursuing personal objectives. And with few exceptions, this is where storytelling in games has remained ever since.

7.4. THE WAY AHEAD

As in every creative profession, improvement is always possible, and for this to happen, designers must learn about storytelling in detail, and keep this in mind throughout the design process. Rather than imposing a host of onerous restrictions, this will offer *endless* pathways for game design creativity, while inducing intensely memorable experiences for your players. The product must remain a game with all of the aspects that make it a game – *but it can also tell a story.* To repeat my 'quick answer'… As long as game designers follow the basic rules of classical storytelling …a prologue, 3D characters with a solid backstory, a clearly defined premise, foreshadowing, a midpoint crisis, failed attempts at resolution, and a final conclusion that resolves the basic conflict and proves the premise – a great story can be told in a game.

One last example...

My goal is a game where players experience a story as deeply as they might experience a terrific movie or novel. Is it possible to weave a powerful story into a game? Can this story make the game substantially greater than the sum of its parts? Has this ever happened? It is one thing to suggest that weaving a powerful story into a game is possible. It is quite another to find a concrete example. In the end, when I saw this happen, I was convinced...

At the heart of the game, *Thief: Deadly Shadows* the player-character is stripped of his unique abilities. To navigate the evil insane asylum known as Shoalsgate Cradle, Garret must rely on wits alone. No horror movie I've ever experienced has instilled as much raw terror or induced such a completely immersive storytelling exper-ience as 'the Cradle,' because here I am, the player-character, buried layers deep, stuck inside this place – and until I figure out the story of this place, I can't leave.

That is when I finally saw just how much storytelling can weave with gameplay to produce something that is greater than the sum of its parts.

The rest of this game isn't so great, and from this, I also realize that storytelling in games isn't going to happen automatically, and it requires a significant and deliberate effort. But for now, if you have any doubts about whether or not storytelling in a game is worth the effort – grab a copy of *Thief: Deadly Shadows*, and work your way through the Cradle. It will be an experience you will never forget.

7.5. SUGGESTIONS FOR HOW TO IMPROVE STORYTELLING IN GAMES

■ A game must remain a game. Just like how a drama can be ruined if too much comedy is injected, a game can't stop to tell its story. Players want to play, and the goal is to discover the story from elements placed inside the game, like overheard dialogue, and hints about the goal of the antagonist.

■ The game should focus on learning about the story – but not like a book. Instead of telling one linear story, build several multithreaded storylines that tell the same story from several perspectives – sort of like a Rashomon structure. While the player moves through the game, the story will be told no matter where the player spends his/her time. The player will experience the story in a unique way, but the structure will remain generally consistent with classical storytelling, no matter how the player travels through the game.

■ Give the player the role of the protagonist, complete with a richly understood backstory. Let her have a boyfriend, a rundown flat, money problems, a complex family history, and other realistic distractions. Don't just pluck your hero off the street, or from some nameless asteroid mining colony, and start them with a convenient case of amnesia.

■ Create a backstory for *all main characters* – not just the protagonist. These people may never get to tell their stories in great detail, but as a game designer, you will begin to see them as genuine personalities, and as a result, you can develop characters who interact and behave realistically.

■ Give minor characters some sort of realistic reason for being there. In the past, non-player characters were mostly slaves, soldiers, or zombies forced into the game without much of a choice. But it's much better if minor characters have their own hopes and dreams …for example, petty pirates scheming for their share of the booty.

■ Create obstacles that are consistent with the dilemma of the story. The antagonist has a plan, and part of this plan requires the antagonist to stand in the way of the player. A deliberate obstruction to the player's quest produces the conflict that drives the story ahead.

■ Establish a fundamentally emotional conflict between the protagonist and antagonist – both of them with a genuine axe to grind. Have the antagonists and their forces resist the player and fight based on who they are, and what they think and believe and want. Don't automate the battles. Give everyone a reason to fight.

■ The ability of the player/protagonist to defeat the antagonist must stem directly from what the player is learning about the antagonist, not through items bought with side-quest game points. And the same way, the antagonist learns about the player/protagonist and reacts according to what the player is doing.

■ Make everything that can happen tie into the story. Perhaps a spaceship is falling apart because the antagonist is a cheap bastard – rather than simply because the game designer thought it would be cool. *Reeeeaaallly* cool elements fit into a story. They are not plopped at our feet.

■ There can be no more random mind-numbing disconnected side-quests placed in the game simply as a way to 'level up.' If at all possible, let the player's growing abilities and playing experience act as the main 'leveling-up' mechanism. The most satisfying rewards are derived from personal skill – not a new suit of armor.

■ Let the main character take a hit that produces a chronic disability. In order to fit the temperature curve, the roleplayed protagonist must experience significant setbacks along the way for legitimate reasons. A constant disability is a great way to help make this happen.

■ As the game progresses, computer-controlled non-player characters (NPCs) must gain abilities based on events and their interactions with the player-character. I know this can introduce run-away instability, and keeping the game balanced when it is self-evolving is one of the hardest tasks in game design. Yet nothing about the story in a game will hold much water if the player is the only one growing based on actual in-game roleplaying experience. If you want to build a game filled with unpredictable and realistic adversaries, check out what is being written on the topic of 'genetic algorithms' and 'machine learning.'

7.6. PARTING SHOT

Success in weaving stories into video games depends on *working* at this craft. If you are committed to building a powerful storytelling experience – don't just skim this topic and set it aside. Review the hardwired rules of storytelling before and during every project.

Good luck, and enjoy the process!

Other Titles by Ken Ramsley

- The Legend of Cyclone Young
- Silver Coins
- The Hive
- The Quality Guy
- Harry James
- Twelve Days to Live
- Porcupine Station

Made in the USA
Coppell, TX
14 January 2022